T5-DGS-545

POLICING:
THE OCCUPATION
AND THE
INTRODUCTION
OF FEMALE
OFFICERS

An Anthropologist's Study

Patricia W. Remmington

LANHAM • NEW YORK • LONDON

Copyright © 1981 by

University Press of America,™ Inc.

4720 Boston Way
Lanham, MD 20706

3 Henrietta Street
London WC2E 8LU England

Library of Congress Cataloging in Publication Data

Remmington, Patricia W. (Patricia Weiser)
    Policing, the occupation and the introduction of female
officers.

    Revision of thesis (Ph.D.)–University of Pittsburgh.
    Bibliography: p.
    1. Atlanta (Ga.)–Police. 2. Policewomen–Georgia
–Atlanta. 3. Law enforcement–Georgia–Atlanta. I.
Title.
HV8148.A7R45   363.2'2'09758231   80–6291
ISBN 0-8191-1646-7   AACR2
ISBN 0-8191-1647-5 (pbk.)

TO MY PARENTS, SOPHIE AND WILLIAM WEISER.

They instilled within me an adven-
turous spirit and the values of
learning, enthusiasm and persever-
ance which helped to inspire the
conception, gestation, labor and
delivery of this study.

iv

CONTENTS

LIST OF TABLES

LIST OF FIGURES

PREFACE

In the summer of 1979, federal and state troops were called into Atlanta, Georgia in order to assist the understaffed local police in combating violent crime rates of near crisis proportions. The media alluded to racial dissension which was allegedly affecting the attitude and productivity of white officers. ·My participant observation with the Atlanta police was conducted earlier-September 1975 to September 1976-but, the findings presented in this book foreshadow and help to explain the breakdown in law enforcement and the subsequent alarming rise in violent crimes. Thus although the general purpose of the study is to describe policing as an occupational subculture and to focus upon the introduction of women, the readers should attain some insight into current conditions in Atlanta specifically.

I would like to extend my gratitude to some of the people who have offered encouragement and assistance in the preparation of this book. My predoctoral field work was funded by the Provost Development Fund of the University of Pittsburgh. Drs. Michael Lowy, Leonard Plotnicov, and Richard Scaglion--my mentors at the Department of Anthropology, University of Pittsburgh each provided invaluable advice and constructive criticism from the research proposal stage to the final thesis. The transition from dissertation to book was expedited and ameliorated by two staff members of the Department of Ethnic Studies, Bowling Green State University--my thanks to Jane Ridenour for her typing and grammatical expertise and to Kay Hanneman for proofing the final manuscript. I am also grateful to my husband, Joseph, and children Jesse and Brian for their presence in my life which acts as kindle for creativity.

My main debt is of course to the officers of the Atlanta Police Department with whom I either rode or spent time. They treated me with kindness and provided candor in both interviews and actions.

INTRODUCTION

Before my first day of participant observation with the Atlanta Police Department was over,
I was warned, "You better not pimp to Reggie."
With that statement, I learned two things quickly--
that I had better learn the language of the
people I was studying; and that I would do well
to keep my mouth shut during my field work. The
translation was, "You better not inform or tell
the police commissioner about anything you see
here" . . . quite a warm welcome to a cultural
anthropologist embarking on twelve months of
research.

A few weeks later, as two officers and I rode
to a call, a sound like a shot was heard. Alarmed,
I turned to the detectives who reassured me that it
was just crazy Mr. McGillicutty who liked to shoot
at cop cars. When we returned to the same area a
few minutes later, the officers reassured me that
Mr. McGillicutty was "a lousy shot." Disbelieving,
I laid down on the floor of the back seat determined that I would not die such an ignominious
death. Again a "shot" was heard accompanied by the
laughter of the detectives who had engineered the
noises by backfiring the car. The initiation was
now completed. For some reason, my unprofessional
behavior and my good natured response to the prank
acted as a key. The formality evoked by an observer ceased; some sort of trust was conceived.
I was now permitted into the private, often illegal
and bizarre world of policing.

The purpose of my field work was to ethnograph-
ically describe policing and focus upon the introduction of women into what was, until recent years,
an all male occupation, often noted in the literature, (Banton 1964: 113; Bittner 1974; Chevigny
1969; Clark 1969: 126-46; Hahn 1974; Levine 1971:
203, 215; Niederhoffer 1969: 229; Patrick 1972;
Rubinstein 1973: 435; Skolnick 1967: 49-62;
Wambaugh 1970, 1972; Westley 1969: 206) for its

intense solidarity and alienation from non-police.

The role of enforcer in a system of laws that are not always equitably administered, and the elements of power and authority inherent in that role, often produce reticence and even hostility from the citizens. The threat of danger and the occupational promotion of cynicism (Niederhoffer 1967, 1969) sustain a suspicion toward outsiders which further isolates the policeman socially. Rubinstein (1973) states that among Philadelphia officers, who are set apart from the public by the above factors and by their irregular hours, there is a strong tendency to find social identity within the squad. The only persons who can fully appreciate an individual's situation are his colleagues. The solidarity that they feel for one another is said by some observers to be a central feature of their personalities. Westley (1970: Foreword) graphically describes the isolating nature of policing.

> The policeman's world is spawned by degradation, corruption and insecurity. He sees man as ill willed, exploitative, mean and dirty, himself a victim of the injustice, misunderstood and defiled.

What rigid boundaries for an outsider to penetrate . . . not only for an anthropologist but also for the females who have joined the policing occupation.

It is not surprising the women, until recently, were channeled into specific assignments separate from the male officers (Breece and Garrett 1974). This was a consequence of two interrelated sets of attitudes: a general stereotype of women as being emotionally and physically weaker than men; and a public concept of law enforcement as a paramilitary institution, involving aggressive and assertive conduct by those who police. Thus, historically the role of women in law enforcement has been characterized by limited opportunities for

2

advancement and by job definitions that have confined women's assignments to areas such as meter
patrols, juvenile work, the processing of women
offenders, and clerical work. This role appears
to have remained virtually unchanged, as reflected
in publications, until the late 1960's (Owings
1969; Rink 1963; Snow 1956; Tenny 1953; Wyles 1952).
The literature published prior to the 1970's conveys an image of policewomen that is "femininely"
based, separate and distinct from the traditionally
"masculine" value system of police work.

In addition to the Civil Rights Act of 1964,
the Crime Control Act of 1973, which prohibits the
recipients of L.E.A.A. (Law Enforcement Assistance
Association) grants from discriminating in employment practices, has encouraged the placement of
female officers in all aspects of police work.[1]
The first females on uniform patrol were introduced in Indianapolis in 1968 (Breece and Garrett
1974: 13). Since the phenomenon has been so
recent, there have been few comprehensive studies
to date. Most of the literature has consisted of
human interest stories in popular magazines, or
statistically oriented resumes of the female
assignment distribution in various departments
(Burnham 1972; Chambers 1973; Horne 1975; Trujillo
1973). The major studies, funded by the Police
Foundation (Bloch and Anderson 1974; Milton 1972,
1974), were preliminary reports based upon quantitative measures such as arrest rates, absentee
rates, and superior officers' ratings. These eval-
uations concluded that: (1) women operate effectively on patrol duty; (2) the public has generally
responded favorably to female officers on patrol;
and (3) male officers have responded negatively
and tend to be overprotective of female officers.

----

[1]One billion dollars a year is awarded in
grants to some 40,000 police departments, courts,
juvenile agencies, and other law enforcement programs by the L.E.A.A.

Studies of female officers in New York City
(Greenwald and Connolly 1974; Sichel, et al. 1977)
also concluded that women performed efficiently on
patrol and that the public generally rated them as
competent.

Given the omnipresent sex-typing of occupations, (Albrecht, Bahr and Chadwick noted in their
1977 study that both sexes in their sample agreed
that many occupations, including detectives were
more suitable for men), and given the solidarity
of the all male group, I was interested in focusing
upon the introduction of women into policing.

Initially, I worked all three shifts. Fewer
calls, both emergency and routine, occurred on day
watch and during the early morning hours of morning
watch. The presence of more superior officers and
administrators, and the daylight on the day watch,
promoted more police-oriented work such as patrolling. After the bars closed and the radio was
"full of dead air" (absence of police calls),
sleeping was not uncommon on morning watch. Therefore, evening watch, considered by most officers as
the most dangerous and active shift, was selected
as the most desirable work shift to study during my
six months with the uniform division. The description of uniformed officers' activities and the
computation of numbers of calls and time spent in
policing duties is thus a view of evening watch
officers only.

For the first two months of the field work I
was relegated to the back seat of the car, since
most detectives in the Sex Crimes and Homicide
squads operate in two-man cars. The opportunities
for actual participation were therefore limited.
However, this time period permitted familiarization
with police routine, formal police terminology
(e.g., signals and codes) and the officers' distinctive slang and jargon. For the remainder of
the year I was permitted to perform as a pseudopartner, especially in the uniform division where
most patrol cars are "one man." (This term is an
expression which is part of the department jargon.

4

Man should be interpretted generically to include women). The officers seemed to enjoy a respite from report writing and victim interrogation and welcomed my participation.

The length of the field work, my eagerness to assist with paper work, my police identification card worn at all times, and the fact that I carried a radio facilitated acceptance by officers who frequently introduced me to both officers and members of the public as a police officer. After six months of field work, my pseudo-police status was exemplified when my "partner" left me guarding the perpetrator of a domestic homicide (a somewhat ambivalent occasion for me). At the officers' instigation I had a .38 caliber pistol in my purse at all times which was illegal but as the officers said, "Who's going to arrest you?" The gun belonged to a detective who had acquired it during a drug bust and had not reported its existence to superiors. Several officers took me to the police practice range where I received several hours of instruction in shooting. Throughout the year I was nicknamed "half-police" (officers pronounced pō'lice as it is spoken in black English).

My rather friendly reception, over time, by the officers may have also been due to the political climate. At the time of my field work, the Atlanta Bureau of Police Services[2] had a black Commissioner of Police. This situation, along with other changes discussed in Chapter 3, had resulted in unusual political conditions and low morale among white police officers. The commissioner had followed a course of reverse discrimination in hiring and promoting policies. His actions had caused a plethora of lawsuits and had frequently been overturned in federal courts.

---

[2]The name Atlanta Bureau of Police Services was introduced in late 1975 to replace the previous designation, Atlanta Police Department. Since both terms were used by the officers, they will be used interchangeably throughout this study.

For example, at the onset of this study, an oral sergeants' examination was given. Over 90 percent of the promotions were awarded to black officers. A deep racial fissioning within the bureau and an almost total white estrangement from the macrostructure were manifested daily by the officers' behavior and by their verbal protests and proclamations of disloyalty. These marked behavioral and attitudinal effects follow Hahn's assertions (1974: 23) that police officers, more than any other occupational group, are apt to personalize authority in departmental superiors and that top administrators can have an important impact on morale or performance of law enforcement organizations.

Thus, throughout the year the officers frequently voiced frustration and disappointment with their jobs, often referring to policing in the "good old days." They no longer felt either judicial or departmental support for their actions and had to exercise much more restraint than in the past. They seemed to welcome someone who could serve as a sounding board for their grievances. Due to the pervasive dissatisfaction which often appeared to outweigh police paranoia, it is possible that this researcher was permitted to see and hear more about the reality of policing.

The sergeant or lieutenant usually assigned my partner for the watch at roll call. Unfortunately, few superior officers placed me with black males. Therefore, this study is largely a reflection of the white segment of the Atlanta Police Bureau. The superior officers did acquiesce to my request to ride with the same officer for several watches. The average time I spent with an officer was four shifts. The rationale was to establish a degree of rapport prior to interviewing. It should be noted that due to the length of my stay at each squad or zone (precinct), I was ultimately assigned to almost every white officer on the shift. The nightly assignment was often based upon which officer was riding alone since one or two cars in each zone would be manned by two officers. Due to these factors, the selection of those observed and interviewed was a rela-

tively random process although black males were
largely excluded.

The year of fieldwork was divided in the following way:

October 1975, Sex Crimes Detectives--
Worked all three watches (one week on
days, one week on evenings, two weeks
on morning watch).

November 1975, Homicide Detectives--
Worked all three watches (two weeks
on days, one week on evenings, one
week on mornings).

December 1975, Robbery Detectives--
Worked first half of month on days,
second half on evening watch.

January 1976, Zone 2 Uniform--Worked
evening watch, 3 p.m. - 11 p.m.

February-Mid-March 1976, Zone 5
Uniform--Worked evening watch, 3 p.m.
- 11 p.m.

Mid-March-April 1976, Zone 1 Uniform--
Worked evenings, 3 p.m. - 11 p.m.

May-June 1976, Zone 3 Uniform--
Worked evenings, 3 p.m. - 11 p.m.

July 1976, Fugitive Detectives--
Worked days, (8 a.m. - 4 p.m.) for
two weeks.

August 1976, Narcotics Detectives--
Worked 10 a.m. - 6 p.m.

September 1976, In-House--Conducted
interviews.

The fifty officers interviewed were drawn from
those with whom I rode for several nights or with

Interview Sample by Sex and Race

	Female	Male	Total
White	10	35	45
Black	3	2	5
Total	13	37	50

Table 1

Interview Sample by Assignment

	Uniform	Plainclothes	In-House	Total
Females				
White	4	3	3	10
Black	1	1	1	3
Males				
White	15	19	1	35
Black	1	1	0	2
Total	21	24	5	50

Table 2

whom I had frequent contact. For example, several
officers assigned to Grady Hospital were questioned.
Although I had never worked with them, our contacts
were frequent during working hours since rape victims, drunk drivers, and injured victims and perpetrators were brought to the hospital. The tables
presented throughout are based upon these fifty
informants. Qualitative information about policing
was also gathered from other officers not formally
interviewed. These included officers I rode with
but did not interview, a male officer who had resigned and was working as a bartender, a female
recruit who became a good friend, and other members
of the bureau frequently encountered during working
hours or whom I saw socially outside of the department. Although they do not constitute a part of the
quantitative sample, these officers assisted immeas-
urably in orienting me to what being a police
officer means--both on and off duty.

Interviews were conducted in as informal a
manner as possible. Locations varied from a moving
police car to a cocktail lounge. The length of the
interview ranged from two to ten hours dependent
upon interruptions by radio calls. The larger number of detectives in the sample reflects their
greater amount of free time on duty.

The Setting

The population of the Atlanta metropolitan
area grew from 1,211,000 in 1966 to 1,577,500 in
1976.[3] Atlanta has also grown as a center for
conventions, entertainment, finance, manufacturing,

---

[3]Population figures are from the Atlanta
Regional Commission. Unfortunately, other census
data for Atlanta, such as socio-economic breakdown,
includes areas of the city that are not policed by
the Atlanta Bureau. These suburban areas generally
appear to be more affluent. They are policed by
county agencies.

retail trade, services, sports, and transportation.
Due to its geographic location, the city is a
focus of government activity. It is the county
seat of Fulton County, the state capital, and the
location of regional offices for many federal
agencies. The second and third largest state
universities in Georgia are found in the Atlanta
region.

Along with the above traits, Atlanta has
taken on a number of other characteristics common
to large urban areas. During the early 1970's it
had one of the highest homicide and rape crime
rates in the United States (based upon 1974 per
capita crime rates). Organized crime, at both a
local and national level, has been found to proli-
ferate in Atlanta. Many organizations headquartered
outside Georgia have interests in the area that include commercial gambling, pornography, prostitution,
narcotics, securities and commercial frauds, and
infiltration of legitimate businesses by organized
crime. Police sources believe that the location
of a federal penitentiary in Atlanta, which has
housed a number of notorious syndicate figures,
has played a major role in attracting organized
crime. The rapid economic development in the
Atlanta region has undoubtedly also contributed to
a rise in all types of criminal activity.

Suburban areas, also considered a part of
Atlanta, are policed by county agencies. The
"white flight" from the metropolitan area has
resulted in a large percentage of blacks residing
in the area patrolled by the Atlanta Police Department. To the officers, it often appears to be an
almost entirely black population, since most of
their calls involve the black populace (see Table
3).

Figure 1 depicts the area policed by the
Atlanta Bureau of Police Services. It is divided
into beats; all beats with the same first digit
belong to the same zone. Most of the calls ree
ceived by detectives and uniformed officers during
the year of observation were in lower-class and

10

1975 Violent Crimes in Atlanta

Crime	Total No.	Victims		Perpetrator		
		White	Black	White	Black	Unknown
Rape	433	113	330	45	397	1
Aggravated Assault	3,518[a]	832	2,462	632	2,662	224
Homicide	185	38	147	23	134	28
Total	4,146	983	2,939	700	3,193	253

Table 3

Source: Atlanta Bureau of Police Services, Planning and Research

[a]Race of victims unknown in 224 cases.

Atlanta Police Beat Districts

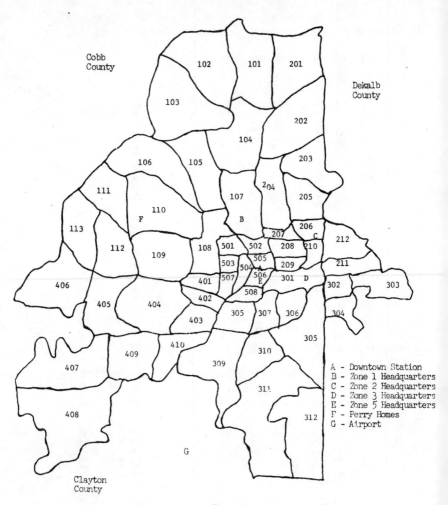

Figure 1

lower-middle-class neighborhoods. The northern sections of the city (beats 101-103; 201 and 202) are affluent and contain the most elite housing in the city. Fewer calls were received from these areas. Government housing projects abound throughout the rest of the city. Beats that contained a project were considered by the officers to be the most dangerous. The largest project, Perry Homes, which is indicated on the map, always had a two-man car patrolling. The downtown section (beats 501-508) includes businesses, hotels, convention facilities, Underground Atlanta (several blocks of shops, restaurants, and bars located below street level), several projects, and the mission district which harbors the urban nomads--tramps, hobos, and winos. Zone 3 (beats 301-312) was considered by most of the Atlanta police officers as the highest risk area of the city.

To the tourist passing through Atlanta, the city appears to be a clean, modern metropolis with attractive landscaping, towering skyscrapers, and a pleasant, moderate climate. To most white Atlanta police officers, the city has lost its aesthetic charm. They see the sections of the city that neither the sightseers nor the commuting business people see. The officers witness the aftermath of crime, the filth and crowded conditions of poverty, the vomit from the drunks and the poliferation of prostitution, narcotics, and pornography. Few white police officers choose to live in the city. The commissioner proposed an ill-fated plan which would have required all members of the bureau to live within the area of the Atlanta policed by the department. Most said that if compelled to live there, they would resign.

STRUCTURE AND DYNAMICS

In order to adequately describe the policing occupation and the incorporation of female officers, it is necessary to understand the general structural plan and organizational dynamics of the Atlanta Bureau of Police Services. This chapter will provide a brief explanation of how the macrostructure operates. Although as Table 4 indicates, in 1976 women constituted less than ten percent of the total police personnel, each division and section shown in Figure 2 had female officer representation. However, due to the recency of female incorporation, there was no female deputy director, major, captain, or lieutenant. Thus, none of the units described below were headed by women. The organizational plan as depicted in Figure 2 was slightly modified in 1976. The changes will be discussed in Chapter 3.

Public Safety Commissioner

E. Reginald Eaves originated and took this post in 1974. He was selected by the black mayor of Atlanta, Eaves's law school roommate. His prior experience in law enforcement was restricted to the penal system of Massachusetts. Eaves's main line of communication to the officers is the daily bulletin and other policy circulars. The former is a newssheet that publicizes transfers, promotions, police athletic events, and "Officer of the Week" and "Officer of the Month" awards. Nominated by the superior officers, the officer(s) of the month is invited to a dinner with the commissioner. Eaves has also set up hours during the week during which any officer can see him about grievances or problems.

Eaves is a very controversial figure. Upon assuming office, he demoted many of the previous administration's hierarchy. This resulted in a

Atlanta Police Personnel by Sex and Race

	Number	Percent
Total in Bureau	1,335	100.0
White		
Male	864	65.0
Female	58	4.3
Total	922	69.0
Black		
Male	342	22.6
Female	71	5.0
Total	413	31.0
Total Male	1,206	90.5
Total Female	129	9.5

Table 4

Note: September 1976 statistics

16

1975 Atlanta Police Department Organizational Plan

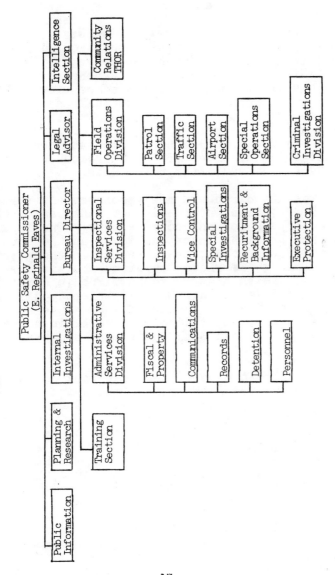

Figure 2

mass of lawsuits. Many of the suits have been successful, resulting in restoration of rank and retro-
active pay. One individual had been an assistant
chief under Chief Inman, Eaves's predecessor. (Any
rank above captain is a delegated position without
tenure security.) After Inman was deposed, the
assistant chief was demoted to lieutenant and assigned to the target range, acknowledged widely as
a place in which to hide one's political enemies.
The state supreme court reinstated him to the rank
of captain and he was placed in charge of a uniform
squad. On his desk, he placed a nameplate that
read, "<u>Captain</u> A, by order of the Supreme Court."
It was ordered removed after a few days.

Since deputy directors are appointed officials,
the holders are viewed by the lesser ranks as mouth-
pieces and puppets for the commissioner. One is in
charge of the Criminal Investigations; another super-
vises the Uniform Patrol; the third is in charge of
the Administrative Services Division; and the last
oversees sections such as Personnel, Public Affairs,
and Planning and Research. One black deputy director has been the butt of almost as much white resentment as Eaves. Implicated in several in-house
scandals, he has evaded both indictment and suspension.

Five of the ten majors, the next rank down,
are black. One directs those sections which fall
directly under Eaves: two are assigned within the
Administrative Services Division; two aid in super-
vision of CID; four majors are assigned to management of the Uniform Division; and one is placed
within the Career Development Division. Therefore,
the commissioner's appointees are scattered throughout the bureau helping the flow of power reach all
ranks and assignments.

Other points of contention between Eaves and
the white police personnel have been his promotion
and transfer policies (discussed at the end of
this chapter) and his restrictions of police power
which will be focused upon in Chapter 3.

Public Information and Planning and Research

These sections are in-house with no street duties. They are directly responsible to (fall directly under) the commissioner. Officers assigned to all in-house administrative positions except Communications work only day watch (8 a.m. - 4 p.m.) and have Saturdays and Sundays off. Public Affairs (three officers)[1] accumulates and disseminates the crime and personnel statistics. Planning and Research (seven officers) writes proposals both for government grants and for modifications within the bureau.

Internal Investigations, Legal Advisor, and Intelligence

Internal Investigations (eleven officers) is the "Pimp" (informer) squad. Any citizen or officer with a complaint must come to these detectives or plainclothes officers (PCO's) to file a report. This squad was only created a few years ago. Prior to its conception, an officer's captain handled any complaints. Reports may vary from alleged police brutality to an officer's alleged use of the word "nigger" in conversation with a member of the public. The officer is called in and the complainant's statement is read to him or her. The officer then makes a written response to the allegations. The situation may end there or the officer may come before a board whose composition varies but is reputed to be overly represented by individuals who share the commissioner's and the black public's perspective. The result may be cessation of employment or suspension. The equitability of decisions and sentences has been questioned--again resulting in lawsuits against the Bureau.

---

[1]All personnel figures are from September 1976 statistics. In many sections, these figures do not represent the total manpower since many civilians (236) are employed in in-house positions.

The <u>Legal</u> <u>Advisor</u> office is composed of three attorneys who ostensibly provide support and advice for all members of the department. Again, white officers believe that the legal advisors, functioning directly under Eaves, spend a disproportionate amount of time supporting and advising the commissioner.

<u>Intelligence</u> (sixteen officers) is a top secret squad which handles Atlanta police action against organized crime. Atlanta is believed to be the southeastern center for drug and prostitution organization. It has been suggested that the Intelligence squad lost much manpower under Eaves since too much underworld activity was being detected--thus giving the police department a poor mark in efficiency.

<u>Training</u>, <u>Community</u> <u>Relations</u>, <u>and</u> THOR

Every police officer goes through a period of training. The number of weeks and the type of practical experience has varied from class to class. Some time is always spent with lectures that describe police procedure. Classes are also held in the martial arts, although many females believe that this aspect of training should be more extensive. One week is spent at the firing range, concluding with qualifying tests. Nine officers are permanently assigned to the training section. Officers from other squads also teach particular classes to the recruits. After classes, the recruits spend several months going from zone to zone, partnered with an experienced officer.

Upon graduation, each officer receives an assignment. Until recently, the students filled out "dream sheets" containing their top three preferred assignments. Apparently, these requests often went unheeded. Officers joke about both the inadequacy of their training and the initial placement of individuals. Prior experience and capabilities are not often considered as criteria for assignments. Thus, a female with several years of experience working as a civilian with crime prevention may find herself alone in a beat car, morning watch (11 p.m. - 7 a.m.), in a high crime area. On the other hand, some females are assigned to detective positions as PCO's immediately after training which has engendered male hostility.

The training section is also responsible for the Physical Fitness Program begun April 1, 1975. All sworn members of the bureau are tested on a semiannual basis. All officers must meet the requirements of Level III or retake that portion of the examination on a monthly basis until meeting the minimum standards. The Level III performance for an officer of either sex, aged 20-29, is: running a mile in 8½ minutes, forty sit-ups, four pull-ups, and twenty push-ups.

Community Relations (twenty-eight officers) includes Missing Persons, Juvenile, and actual community relations work. PAL, the Police Athletic League, is also part of Community Relations. Police officers can participate in a great variety of sports, from football to golf. The participants are mostly black. Officers are permitted to be late or absent from their regular assignments (and receive regular pay) for sports practices and games. Thus, PAL is often used by dissatisfied officers as a symbol of the current hierarchy's concept of policing--"too much P.R. and not enough police work."

THOR (Target Hardening and Opportunity Reduction - thirty-eight officers) operated until recently under a government grant. It is organized to disseminate literature and advice for the prevention of crime. Among their duties, THOR personnel go from house to house in high crime areas installing new locks, putting identification numbers on household property to aid recovery in the event of theft, and lecturing residents on crime prevention. It is difficult to assess the efficacy of THOR. One victim of an attempted rape had been visited by THOR personnel the same day, and new locks had been installed. Although living in

21

the ground floor apartment, she went to sleep with
the sliding patio door fully open. The sex crimes
detectives noted the THOR sign outside her door.
It appeared to increase the detectives' skepticism
and aloofness from the victim.

Administrative Services Division

Communications is manned by both sworn officers and civilians. The presence of civilians in
the radio section is a source of dissatisfaction
among officers who feel that a civilian, without
"street" experience, cannot adequately execute the
important duties of a radio dispatcher. The radio
is indeed the lifeline of the police officer.
Detective cars have radios, and the detecitves
also carry walkie-talkies when they are outside of
the car. Uniformed officers wear their radios,
the speaker attached near the shoulder. Seven UHF
frequencies are used. Each zone has its own frequency; there is a county-wide frequency used by
specialized units such as the specialized weapon
and tactical squad; an administrative frequency is
used by city and police hierarchy. All detectives
utilize the same VHF frequency.

When someone calls the department, (s)he speaks
to one of the complaint officers who either disposes
of requests for police services or records the call
on dispatch cards which are relayed to the appropriate dispatcher. The card contains the signal(s)
involved and the address. The dispatchers each have
a map before them with lights representing the cars
in service. They give the calls to the nearest in-
service officer, for example, "Radio calling 3204."
("3" refers to evening watch; "2" refers to zone 2;
and "04" is the particular beat.) The dispatcher
then repeats the car number, the address, and the
particular signal, Other numbers may be given,
such as 78 (a description of a suspect) or a code
number that indicates urgency. The dispatcher may
also direct another car to go with 3204. The
police officer repeats the information. Upon
arrival at the address, the officer contacts radio,

saying that "3204 is 26." Upon completion of the call, (s)he again notifies the dispatcher with the proper code, for instance, code 17, "report has been taken." The dispatcher then lights up that beat car on the board indicating that it is back in service. (Radio procedures will be dealt with more thoroughly in subsequent chapters concerning the daily routine of police officers.)

Property Management is housed in several offices. At one location officers can sign for ammunition, pens, and other items. At another office, lost or stolen property, evidence, and contents of impounded cars are turned in. The latter can be a time-consuming process. All objects must be listed by the officer as they are removed from the car. Once in the property office, another list must be made as they are handed in. Several reports must also be filled out. Any money must be counted twice by the officer turning it in. It is placed in a sealed envelope and taped with the officer's initials beneath the tape. It is for these reasons that police officers dread having to impound a car a few minutes before their watch would normally end. One might have to be on duty an extra hour just filling out property reports.

The Detention section in the city jail is no longer manned by sworn police officers. Although situated in the older section of police headquarters in downtown Atlanta, it is now run by civilian employees of the city. Eleven police officers do oversee the detention area of Grady Hospital--a mammoth city hospital several blocks from police headquarters. DUI's (driving under the influence) are brought there for alcohol content testing. Persons who appear at all demented also go through Grady Detention. Injured perpetrators are turned over to Grady Detention. Many police personnel view this assignment as a "garbage detail," which may be due to the contact with drunks and the lack of street work.

Inspectional Services Division

The Inspection squad (six officers) drops in unexpectedly at uniform roll calls, at detective offices, and elsewhere. Their purpose is to check the appearance of the officers and their cars. An officer can be "written up" for rather trivial things such as length of sideburns and hair, size of hats, objects found under the back seat of the car, or for wearing combat boots. If Inspectional Services dictates that an officer's hair is too long, the officer's sergeant shares in the responsibility. If the inspector returns and finds that no action has been taken, both the officer and his or her sergeant may be sent home without pay.

Vice Control includes Gambling (thirteen officers), Prostitution (seventeen officers), and Narcotics (twenty-five officers). All officers, prior to promotion to detective rank, used to be assigned to a vice squad for several months. Informant relationships that can be used for years are best cultivated in this squad. The Gambling squad spends most of its time attempting to break up the numbers racket and the corner crap games. The Prostitution squad has been active in disrupting the massive massage parlor operation in Atlanta. Utilizing female officer decoys, it has also concentrated upon arresting the solicitee-the "john." The large number of female impersonators and homosexuals are also dealt with by the Prostitution squad. Any officer who has ever worked in this squad has "war stories" to relate. These usually focus upon the actual arrest of a prostitute, in a hotel room, on a hotel bed. (The Narcotics squad, operating in Metro Atlanta (this includes the outlying county areas) will be discussed in detail in Chapter 4.)

Special Investigations is not actually a formed squad. When a situation arises, possibly internal corruption, that warrants inspection, the commissioner can activate this squad. Apparently this has not occurred in some time since most officers were not even aware of its potential existence.

Recruitment and Background Investigation has
six sworn officers. Due to antidiscriminatory
employment laws, there is no longer a height or
weight requirement for police officers. To qualify
one must be between twenty and thirty-six years of
age, with a high-school diploma or equivalency,
have 20/40 vision, and be physically healthy.
There are no entrance exams or I.Q. tests.

The Background Investigations squad, in plain
clothes, investigates an applicant's past and present. They also administer a polygraph to all
police aspirants. Today, a person with a police
record can be accepted as a potential police officer, although any person who has been convicted of
an aggravated misdemeanor or felony is ineligible.
Prior to Commissioner Eaves's control, any previous
lock-up would have excluded the possibility of
employment. Today, a drunk-and-disorderly conviction is acceptable. Rumors also abound that
several females with records in prostitution have
been hired by the bureau since Eaves has been in
control.

The Executive Protection squad includes those
officers who act as bodyguards or chauffeurs for
the commissioner and the mayor of Atlanta. These
assignments have the reputation of being a step-
ping-stone to higher positions since they involve
a degree of intimacy with the ruling elite.

Field Operations Division

Field Operations can be divided into two sections: the uniform patrol and the detectives.
Chapters 4 and 5 discuss the day-to-day experiences of these groups. Therefore, only a summary
of structure and roles will be presented at this
time.

Uniformed Officers. The Atlanta uniformed
officer is assigned to one of the five zones, to

the airport or Model Cities, or to a special operations squad. Most uniformed officers' shift hours
are either: day, 7 a.m. - 3 p.m.; evening, 3 p.m.
- 11 p.m.; or morning, 11 p.m. - 7 a.m.

Atlanta Police Zones

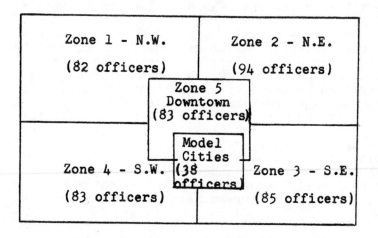

Figure 3

Each of the five zones (precincts) has a headquarters situated within the physical boundaries of
the zone. Most of these precinct buildings are old
and contain only two or three rooms. These headquarters are also changed to other building sites
periodically. The largest room in the zone headquarters is the location of roll call at the
beginning of each watch. Each zone has one captain
who works Day Watch hours; one lieutenant and three
sergeants for each of the three watches; and approximately fifteen to twenty officers working each
watch.

The zone is divided into two sectors. Each
sector is also divided into five or six beats.
Each sector has an "umbrella" car--the entire sector is that car's beat. The watch change for the

umbrella cars is either fifteen minutes before or after the watch ends for the other cars. Thus there is always a car on patrol. The highest risk beats have two-man cars (one or two beats per zone). An officer either has a regular beat or is a "rousta-bout," taking over beat cars on officers' off-days (Department jargon for days off); or an officer may be the regular paddy-wagon driver transporting per-petrators to the city jail. The patrolman is responsible for: (1) the protection of life and property, the prevention and detection of crime, the apprehension and arrest of violators and the reduction of crime on his assigned beat by patrol-ling and observing; (2) (S)he must acquaint himself with all streets, alleys, courts, and buildings within the limits of his beat; (3) (S)he should become acquainted with as many people in the beat as possible; (4) (S)he must keep informed as to locations of frequent crimes; (5) (S)he must learn the identity of "police characters" living in and frequenting the beat. These are some of the re-sponsibilities for field officers as outlined in the Procedural Guideline. However, there is a gap between theory and practice.

Due to off-days, there are usually only two sergeants per watch at each zone. Each has respon-sibility for one sector and are referred to as "Sector A sergeant" and "Sector B sergeant." The sergeant is considered responsible for the appear-ance and performance of his officers. In order to supervise the sector, a sergeant must see that his "men" remain in their assigned beats, regulate the eating periods, and make sure that the officers do not remain an unnecessary length of time at one location. The discretion that sergeants use in enforcing these rules has produced a great deal of intra-zone conflict (see Chapter 5). Sergeants are fond of telling everyone that they know and understand the patrol officers who work with them. Most sergeants express the belief that they know where their officers are at all times, including their deviant activities. There is some doubt that this is true, judging by the actual rule infrac-tions that are constantly taking place. The zone sergeant has other duties: he issues subpoenas;

conducts roll call training twice a week; assigns off-days, presumably on the basis of seniority; collects, reviews, and approves any reports taken during the watch; and is supposed to accompany his officers on as many calls as possible.

The zone watch lieutenant appears to be present mostly as a supervisor of the sergeants' activities. He ensures that they are managing their sectors efficiently and are keeping adequate records on the personnel. The lieutenant should be available to advise and accompany sector sergeants on situations and calls. He is also the liaison between the zone commander and all underlings. He must keep the captain aware of all unusual situations occurring within the zone.

The zone captain's role is not outlined in any procedural guideline issued by the department. They are rarely seen or heard from by the uniformed officers. Three of the five zone captains are black. No interviewed officer understood the exact nature of the zone captains' position, although most felt that the captains spent a large amount of police time in private pursuits.

Uniformed officers are also assigned to Model Cities. Formed in 1975, it took over several beats from zones 3, 4, and 5. These beats, located near the Atlanta Stadium, contained several housing projects and the highest crime rates in the city. A new approach in policing is employed in the Model Cities project: team policing. The uniformed officer also performs the normal functions of the detectives and the ID unit (see below). (S)he follows a case through the entire investigation instead of turning the reports into Criminal Investigations.

Seventy-nine officers are assigned to the airport. Although it does not lie within the city boundaries, the airport is policed by the bureau. It is considered another "garbage" assignment by most personnel.

Special Operations includes many squads that utilize uniformed personnel: Motormen, ID, High

Crime Foot Patrol, SWAT, and Rescue. The Motor-cycle squad's function is not clearly delineated. Ideally, motorcycle officers should handle auto-mobile accidents and traffic, since motorcycles can more easily proceed through congested traffic. But the beat officer handles most wrecks while the motormen (or women, since there are two females assigned to this squad) handle many traffic viola-tions and special details. Until 1974, there were uniform cars that only handled traffic. Today these duties are divided between the beat cars and the motormen.

The ID unit, made up of civilians and sworn officers, is kept busy in Atlanta. They check for prints at crime scenes (homicide, rape, and bur-glary) and thoroughly examine all stolen and im-pounded cars.

High Crime Foot Patrol works different hours than other uniformed officers. Their watch changes occur at 10 a.m., 6 p.m., and 2 a.m. They walk a small beat area in the downtown district including Underground Atlanta, the infamous Auburn Street (black vice center), the equally infamous Peachtree Street (white vice center), and the area around the mission which is heavily populated by skid-row drunks. Most signal 63's (officer in trouble) come from these officers who are on foot. They are quickly backed up by beat cars.

SWAT (Special Weapons and Tactical unit) is employed when hostages are involved; during a house-to-house search; with a shoot-out or sniper; or when a bomb or bomb threat is involved. SWAT officers also back up other beat cars particularly in Zone 3, the highest risk area. SWAT is con-sidered by most officers to be a special assignment which should ideally be composed of the most compe-tent police officers. Both SWAT and motorcycle per-sonnel do appear to consider themselves members of elite squads.

Rescue is the police-run paramedic unit. It appears at many calls when injuries are involved.

However, the ambulance service from Grady Hospital seems to arrive at least concurrently with the police rescue car. Officers working in this squad have received approximately eighty hours of medical training.

Criminal Investigations Division. This section encompasses field operations personnel who are either detectives (a rank above uniformed officer) or plainclothes officers (PCO's are the same rank as uniform). Detective squads include: Homicide (twenty-two officers), Robbery (twenty officers), Sex Crimes (eleven officers), Burglary (seventeen officers), Larceny (sixteen officers), Checks (five officers), Auto Theft (twenty officers), and Fugitive (twelve officers). Special Operations squads include: Anti-Robbery (forty-five officers), Anti-Burglary (forty-three officers), and School detectives (seventeen officers).

Each detective squad has a lieutenant who usually works the day watch. Each watch also has a detective sergeant, although only Homicide, Robbery, and Sex Crimes have a morning watch operating. These superior officers' duties are similar to those outlined above for uniformed superiors. But rarely does one see a detective sergeant or lieutenant on the street despite the portrayal of sergeants and lieutenants in the mass media. Captains, majors, and a deputy director also supervise the activities of the CID squads.

The actual performance of three detective squads will be discussed in Chapter 4. Therefore, only a brief role summary will be presented here. The outlined duties of detectives include: (1) responding to a uniformed officer's request for the presence of a detective of a particular squad; (2) investigating reports that were originally taken by uniform, passed through Report Review and assigned by the detective sergeant to a particular detective; (3) and patrolling the streets in order to deter and detect crimes. Most detectives' watch hours differ from uniform (day, 8 a.m. - 4 p.m.; evening, 4 p.m. - 12 a.m.; morning, 12 a.m. - 8 a.m.). The rationale is that there should always be police on the street.

The detectives' beat is the entire city of Atlanta.
Due to this geographical space and to the fact that
detectives do not have to inform radio of their constant whereabouts, detectives have much more freedom than uniformed officers. Each of the detective
squads operates somewhat autonomously. Although
most are located on the third floor of the station,
there is little contact between squads. There
appears to be much camaraderie within the detective
squad, although, once again, with a distinct racial
schism.

Homicide, considered by many as the elite
squad, handles killings, suicides, aggravated
assaults, and arson. Sex Crimes deals with cases
of rape, child molestation, sodomy, exhibitionism,
and voyeurism. Robbery investigates cases where
property was taken by force or threat of force.
Burglary handles cases where property was stolen
from a building without the cognizance of the owner.
Burglary detectives are also assigned to several of
the zones and follow up all burglary reports taken
in that zone. Larceny detectives investigate cases
of theft by taking (without force). Checks handles
forgery cases, and Auto Theft works on the vast
number of stolen cars in Atlanta. Fugitive, considered by most officers as a high risk position,
searches for escaped prisoners and those wanted for
questioning by the other squads.

Anti-Robbery squad personnel either function
as stake-out teams in stores with a high incidence
of robberies, or they act as decoys, impersonating
drunks who are likely targets for robbery. Anti-
Burglary includes the helicopter squad that patrols
businesses from the sky, locating open doors and
fleeing perpetrators for the beat cars; they are
also involved in undercover fencing operations in
which they set up purchases of stolen goods. The
School Detectives act as surveillance teams for
the city's schools. They also investigate bur-
glaries and cases of malicious mischief in schools.

Uniformed officers, detectives, and superior
officers may be assigned to other offices not discussed in this brief summary. These include the

31

Courts, Maintenance, Pawnshop, Permits, Traffic office, Transportation, Records, and Fiscal squads.

It should be noted that aside from the racial division in the Atlanta Police Department and the tension between superior officers and the uniformed or detective officer, there is also antagonism between the uniformed officers and the detectives. The former believe that detectives do very little work yet receive most of the accolade and credit. For instance in the case of a signal 50/48 (shooting, dead person) although the uniformed officer is the first one on the crime scene, and may perhaps apprehend the perpetrator, it is the homicide detective who fills out the arrest reports and receives the statistical credit for the arrest. The detectives, on the other side, often view the uniformed officer as an inferior. They are frequently maligned by detectives--accused of ineptitude, causing disruption of the crime scene (e.g. they touch a weapon and ruin the fingerprints). Uniformed officers are also either accused of calling for a detective when his presence is not actually necessary or of not contacting a detective when the situation warranted. Much of this inter-rank antagonism may be traced to the downward mobility paranoia of the detective and the upward mobility aspirations of the uniformed officer.

A. Mobility Within the Structure

Downward mobility, demotion, has already been alluded to. Officers are always aware of the potential drop in salary and prestige. Plain-clothes officers assigned to detective squads are particularly wary of returning to uniformed assignments. They have experienced the relative freedom that detectives enjoy.

The promotion system is the most controversial issue within the department at this time. Prior to Eaves, there was no formal promotional examination or system. Upward mobility was the result of influence or nepotism. If a particular individual was promoted to captain, several of his protegees moved up the hierarchy with him. The percentage of black superior officers was quite low, since the power structure and flow was white.

At first, Eaves devised a written examination. Test scores were added to other scores based upon education, tenure, and other factors. The result was that a large number of white officers were promoted. Examinations since then have been oral, held before a committee designated by the commissioner. The first oral test (October 1975) resulted in the advancement of twenty-nine detectives to sergeant rank. Twenty-four were black officers, including two black females. Several of these new sergeants had little or no actual street experience. Their promotion to supervisory positions offended many white officers who believed themselves to be better qualified. The new sergeants, known as "Reggie's Sergeants," have created near crisis conditions at the zones by upsetting the status quo with their exercise of power.

The only female sergeants in 1976 were two black women who received their promotions as a result of the October 1975 exam. Their advancement caused a great deal of anger and frustration among white male officers for three reasons: they were black; they were women; and neither had been with the bureau for more than three years.

As Table 5 shows, the percentage of black superior officers is almost equivalent to the total percentage of black officers in the bureau. But this mathematical equivalency represents a degree of reverse discrimination in the promotional system in order to compensate for the years of discrimination against blacks. Thus the examination system seems farcical to most white officers. Presently denied the reward incentive for excellent police work, the vast majority of white officers are just going through the motions of policing.

Many are either applying for other jobs or are furthering their education with an eye towards federal or state law enforcement. Education is encouraged by L.E.A.A., which pays not only for

Personnel by Rank, Sex, Race

RANK	White		Black		
	Male	Female	Male	Female	Total
Director	1	0	0	0	1
Deputy Director	2	0	2	0	4
Major	5	0	5	0	10
Captain	21	0	9	0	30
Lieutenant	46	0	9	0	55
Sergeant	94	0	63	2	159
Detective	127	3	65	4	199
Plainclothes Police Officer	21	7	14	3	45
Police Officer	546	48	176	62	832
Total	864	58	342	71	1,335

Table 5

tuition and supplies but also gives the police officer an allowance. College education also results in increased pay as indicated in Table 6. The officers frequently complain that their salaries are too low, often voicing their opinion that this reflects society's poor image of police officers. Most Pittsburgh police, 89.5 percent, also felt that their pay was inadequate for their needs (Scaglion 1973: 46). Many Atlanta officers, as discussed in Chapter 4, supplement their income by working extra jobs that are usually police related.

There is also a great deal of horizontal movement within the police department. Daily bulletins often contain long lists of transfers. Some transfers are the result of the individual officer's request. An officer may submit a written transfer request to the commissioner; it may be accepted or rejected. The rationale behind other transfers is not clear. One sergeant had supervised a zone sector, evening watch, for over a year. His rapport and relationship with the officers were excellent. He was then transferred to another zone without any warning. Two more position changes occurred in the next two months. Finally, he was put back in his original assignment. Transfer actions go up the chain of command to the Affirmative Action officer. It is the duty of this office to maintain the appropriate race and sex proportions in all zones and squads. Therefore, if a white male is transferred from a certain watch at Zone 2, a white male must replace him if the previous race/sex balance was correct. The affirmative action plan and racial proportions demanded by government grants have caused much resentment, since the best qualified may not be chosen. One example was the necessity of putting a female officer on the SWAT team. Most males sincerely do not believe that any female can perform the tasks of this highly specialized squad as adequately as men can.

Officers may also have their beats changed at the discretion of the sector watch sergeant or the lieutenant. Several of the recently promoted

35

Salary Range by Rank

Years in Dept.	Uniform H.S. Degree	Uniform 2 yrs. college	Detective/ Uniform 4 yrs. college	Sergeant	Lieutenant	Captain	Major	Deputy Director	Director
1st year	10,049	10,465	10,907	11,362	12,844	14,313	16,913	19,162	27,872
2nd year	10,465	10,907	11,362	11,830	13,377	14,924	17,628	19,981	29,068
3rd year	10,907	11,362	11,830	12,324	13,936	15,561	18,832	20,826	30,316
4th year	11,362	11,830	12,324	12,844	14,521	16,224	19,162	21,710	31,616
5th year	11,830	12,324	12,844	13,377	15,132	16,913	19,981	22,633	32,968
6th year	12,324	12,844	13,377	13,936	15,769	17,628	20,826	23,595	34,372
7th year[a]	12,844	13,377	13,936	14,521	16,432	18,832	21,710	24,596	35,828

Table 6

[a] Remain at same salary after 7 years unless promoted or entire department given a raise.

sergeants have moved many officers out of "their" beats. This caused tension to grow within the zone. An officer's beat can become a second home to him. He knows many of the residents; he has established places where he is assured free coffee and he is aware of the half-price hasheries within the beat which, although forbidden, are still very common; and he has his secret places where he is able to elude the eyes of superior officers and pursue private activities. Then, without prior warning, his name may either appear on the transfer list or, at his sergeant's caprice, his beat is changed.

B. Voluntary Associations

The racial division in the Atlanta Police Department is reflected in the three organizations that have formed as voluntary associations. The Fraternal Order of Police is almost entirely white. The Afro-American Patrolman's League prohibits any white members. A third organization, the Police Benevolent Association, formed in September 1975, has attempted to bridge the racial division in order to represent a unified whole for bargaining and demands. None of these associations are unions since police officers are forbidden by law to unionize. All function as fraternal organizations that gather dues and provide mutual aid, such as legal defense, and advice to the members. The aid aspect has been utilized extensively in the last few years with the plethora of lawsuits arising from demotions and suspensions.

This chapter has attempted to show how complex and elaborate the structure of a police department is. Women have been incorporated into all parts of the organization by assignment. Chapters 7 and 8 will examine how successful this incorporation has actually been. The Atlanta Police Department is more decentralized than a small town police department would be. But the power structure is very apparent and the commissioner's presence is felt in every zone and office. The structure is being threatened at this time by severe racial division.

Every officer is aware of the "politics" of the bureau. And almost every white male officer inter- viewed expressed feelings of frustration at his inability to move upward through the structure. For example, the following are some answers to the question, "What is it like for you being a police officer?"

> I like my work but don't like where I'm working or who I'm working for. It's run crappy. (white male, Uni- form, age 23)

> It's not as close as it used to be. At this point in time, it's a job. Two or three years ago it would have been a lot different. (white male, Detective, age 30)

> It's enjoyable because I believe in law and order and it allows me to get out and help maintain it . . . want to help change the image of the depart- ment and show the people that we're here to help them. (black male, Uniform, age 27)

Let us now look at Chapter 3 in order to understand the changes that have led to the present structure and political climate in Atlanta.

3

CHANGES OVER TIME

The structure of the Atlanta Police Department
has never been rigid. It is, however, within the
last thirty years that dynamic changes have occurred
within both the structural organization and the
style of policing. In the first twenty-five years
of this period (1947-1972) the department was
directed by one individual, Chief Herbert Jenkins.
When he assumed the leadership of the department,
it had relatively few personnel (526) and was con-
trolled by the Ku Klux Klan influence in the police
union (Mathias and Anderson 1973). Jenkins first
disbanded the union membership. Having rid the
department of the conservative influences, Jenkins
began to initiate measures to modernize and enlarge
the police force.

Nineteen forty-seven marked the founding of the
Police Training Academy which was designed to offer
a modified version of the FBI training course.
During the same year, the detective department was
reorganized into specialized squads. In 1951, the
entire police department underwent a thorough administrative reorganization into four divisions:
Uniform, Traffic, Detective, and Services. Each
division was placed under the command of a superin-
tendent, thus decentralizing the power and further
specializing the manpower.

What was policing like during the 1950's and
1960's in Atlanta? Listening to officers discuss
the "good old days," the pre-Eaves, pre-black, and
pre-female era, one glimpses the type of police
officer and department portrayed in the mass media
of the present and the past. Until several years
ago, all officers met at downtown headquarters for
roll calls. Everyone knew everyone else. There
was only one radio frequency; hence an officer was
aware of what was occurring throughout the city.
Until 1961 all beat cars were manned by two officers. The sense of camaraderie was strong and
there was little fear that one's fellow officers

would inform to superior officers. Officers felt
trust for one another. They also speak of the
trust and support that they felt from their superiors and the police department as an entirety. If
an officer had a problem with a private citizen, he
felt confident of the allegiance of the department's
hierarchy: "Chief Jenkins would always stand behind his men."

All officers had to meet certain physical qualifications in these "idyllic" policing days. Hence,
an officer felt a sense of security, being assured
of the prowess of partners and others who would
assist him when needed. The general impression
given of policing during that time is therefore
entirely different from the department today. The
racially segregated, all-male police department had
a strong sense of esprit de corps, solidarity, and
security.

In the spring of 1948 black police officers
were hired for the first time. But, to appease the
white population, certain compromise measures were
instituted. Blacks could only patrol in black
neighborhoods and were only authorized to arrest
blacks. Initially, the black officers had a
separate headquarters located in the black YMCA.
They moved into the main station in 1950 but
dressed in separate facilities and had their own
roll calls. Black patrolmen were not permitted to
wear their uniforms or carry police equipment off
duty. They were commanded by white officers.

Over the ensuing years, more blacks joined the
department, and some advanced through the ranks.
In 1961 the first black was promoted to sergeant.
In 1962 black officers were authorized to arrest
whites and in 1965, the degrading practice of
printing separate reports for white and black officers was abolished; the annual report of the department no longer included a "Negro Police Report."
In 1966 the separate watch for blacks was abolished
and they were assigned to regular patrol duty on the
morning and evening watches. At the same time a
black sergeant was assigned to a supervisory role
over both black and white officers. By the late

1960's black and white policemen were working together as partners in an effort to show the people
of Atlanta that the two races could work together.
However, by the mid 70's this portrayal of interracial cohesiveness had ceased, replaced by racial
hostility and interactional separation.

Females have been a part of the Atlanta Police
Department since 1918 when two females were hired
to arrest prostitutes and carry out other duties
such as inspecting rooms where males might encounter
embarrassing situations (Mathias and Anderson 1973:
80). In 1924 a woman's bureau was created within
the department to handle juveniles and nonstreet
work. In 1950, policewomen went on duty to patrol
crosswalks on school days, and in 1957 two females
were assigned walking beats as the first two uniformed policewomen in the history of the Atlanta
police force. But it was not until 1972 that
females entered the Police Academy. That same year,
eight females began uniform duty on the street. The
active participation of females in all facets of
police work is therefore a very recent phenomenon.

Prior to the integration of blacks and females
in the late 1960's and 1970's, the style of policing was apparently quite different. Most information pertaining to the past is revealed in the "war
stories" told over beer at the end of the watch or
during lengthy 59's (officers meeting) where
gripings about the present turn to nostalgic
recollections of the past. War stories are just
that--stories, undoubtedly glorified and exaggerated for police peers and edited for civilian
listeners. Beneath the words, however, one is left
with a strong impression of police power and utilization of police discretion. Blacks, homosexuals,
hippies, and drunks were usually the targets of the
harassment that is recounted in these accounts of
past adventures.

One story illustrates the support previously
offered by superior officers. During the late
1960's many hippies drifted into Atlanta, concen-
trating in a small area of the northeast section of
the city. During the evenings, many gathered at

Piedmont Park, a large city park which today is a center for homosexual activity. Apparently many officers used to while away a summer's evening by going to the park and harassing and manhandling the hippies (referred to as "maggots" by Atlanta police). As a precautionary measure they used tape to cover their badge numbers and car numbers. Several officers remember the day they were called before a captain who sternly informed them that he was aware of these practices and their involvement. Nervously they awaited a suspension or a lengthy lecture. Instead the captain smiled and commended them on their actions. His only admonishment was that they should be careful and not be caught. Variations on this type of story are common. All stress the superior's praise and support for being a true police officer.

The Piedmont Park incidents did not pass unnoticed, however. In 1969 two officers were transferred out of the area around the park. They were accused of having deliberately provoked a clash with a rock music audience. This incident was only one in a long series of incidents and accusations involving the police and the hippie community. The hippies compared Atlanta to Mayor Daley's Chicago, and time after time, they accused the Atlanta police of trying to drive them from their tightly-knit community. This police effort, supplemented by the natural fading of the hippie movement, apparently succeeded since the area that was once the site of numerous "head" shops and discotheques is now the center for blue movies and massage parlors.

When police officers worked in the city jail, they had ideal victims for harassment and brutality --the incarcerated winos. On cold evenings, drunks were stripped and taken outdoors to sing Christmas carols. They were frequently told that their genitals had to be printed for identification. They might also be informed that they had been arrested for various crimes such as rape and were to be punished by death. Aside from such mental harassment, apparently a great deal of physical brutality was exercised by officers working in the jail. In

42

1969 a grand jury investigation into many charges
of police brutality recommended that only selected
officers should work in detention, with a superior
officer present who was adept at handling unruly
prisoners without overreacting. These changes were
instituted but, several years later, all sworn
police officers ceased working in the jail.

Some of the favorite war stories involve the
exploits of a certain officer who has been almost
deified by white officers as a symbol of what
policing used to be like. Among his vast repertoire
of practical jokes, the "funniest" activity of this
officer was to ride around with his partner waiting
for a black person, preferably old, walking a dog.
Officer B would use his rifle and shoot the dog.
The presumed humor of the situation was to watch
the animal owner continue walking unaware of the
dog's death. This officer is also reputed to have
shot at windows of houses and automobiles. His
brutal use of violence is also regaled at length--
the police officer of the past.

Officers speaking about brutality stress the
elation and excitement that it produces. One officer who had worked in the jail and participated in
frequent acts of brutality toward prisoners said
that the frustration of police work produced it.
He felt badly about it retrospectively, but at the
time, "it was natural, sort of."

Much of the police officers' misuse of power
stemmed from the laws, or lack of them, at that
time. Suspects did not have to be informed of
their rights; lengthy interrogations outside and
inside of the police station were commonplace.
Prisoners often arrived at the city jail with marks
that revealed a confrontation with the arresting
officer. The department stood behind the actions
of the men. Nothing was thought of using derogatory ethnic labels; violence and discretion were
aimed at certain groups. The police officer had
power legally and the discretion to use or abuse
it. As Banton (1964) stated, illegal behavior has
proliferated among American police since the solidarity of the officers reduced the supervisors'

power and their ability to eliminate misuse of
power. Westley's 1969 study was also concerned
with the illegal use of violence by police. He
found that officers both accept and morally jus-
tify these practices through occupational experiences.

Ten years ago in Atlanta an officer could
shoot any fleeing felon. Today, he must have observed the perpetrator in the act or be shooting in
self defense. This is just one of the recent
changes in police procedure that, according to the
officers, threaten their safety.

The present administration has introduced
other measures that have affected the officers' use
of weapons and style of policing. Shotguns are now
forbidden. "Inferior" ammunition is prescribed for
service revolvers although many officers do "hot
load" their bullets (add extra powder), contrary to
regulations.

Many police personnel complain about these
changes and feel a distinct loss of security. Any-
time an officer does use his pistol he must come
before a shooting committee. The amount of shooting is quite infrequent today, contrary to mass
media portrayal. Many informants had never shot
their guns in the line of duty--some had rarely, if
ever, drawn them. Today, at least, the use of
weapons is considered to be a last resort. This
appears to be the result of weapon and ammunition
regulations, court decisions, the existence of the
shooting committee and Internal Investigations, and
the change in the general style of policing that
now pervades the Atlanta Bureau of Police Services.

Several legal decisions have had a profound
effect upon policing. The Fourth Amendment, concerning unreasonable searches and seizures, and the
Fifth Amendment, which protected individuals from
coerced confessions and self-incrimination, cur-
tailed the power of the police (Rankin 1972). The
Fourth Amendment also applies to any information
obtained by a police officer through any restraint
he places upon the liberty of a citizen by show of

authority or physical force, whether or not it is an actual arrest. With the Miranda Decision (1966) the Supreme Court held that a confession obtained from an accused at any time after he was taken into custody or otherwise detained would not be admissible unless he had first been informed of his right to remain silent, that anything he said may be held against him, and that he had the right to counsel. These legal decisions have confined the practice of "police brutality" to a great extent.

However, there is still some illegal use of force. Prisoners may still arrive at the jail wearing the infamous "resisting arrest turban," the bandage wrapped around the head for injuries sustained from police use of the slapjack. The legal changes have presented a conflict for police officers which Skolnick (1967) summarizes. It is a conflict between maintaining the social order on the one hand and the existence of a set of laws emphasizing the rights of the individual and constraints upon the initiative of law enforcement agents on the other side. This situation, producing tension and frustration has become more intense in recent years. One resolution to the conflict appears to be the redefinition of the role of police officer from law enforcer to peace-keeper and public relations officer--an image that many officers feel the present administration is trying to project.

Aside from judicial decisions, changes in policing have also been the result of the changing physical characteristics of officers. Equal rights regulations have eliminated physical qualifications. Many older officers complain about the "weaklings" now accepted by the department and their fears of being unable to receive adequate backup. The mere presence of women in uniform, involved in all aspects of police work, has of course affected the past physical image of virility and strength of the officers as an entirety.

Lastly, the rise of blacks into all positions of leadership, including that of commissioner, has affected how the white officers feel about support from the hierarchy and from all those assigned to

their squad or zone. The mid-sixties brought integration to the Atlanta Police Department. Between
January 1973 and March 1975, there was a 7.8 percent
increase in number of black officers (Law Enforcement Assistance Association Office of Civil Rights
Compliance). However, separation still exists both
socially and professionally. Upon entering the
precinct building prior to roll call, one rarely
sees black and white officers conversing. The room
is almost invisibly divided. There are a few excep-
tions. Each zone or detective squad has one or two
black members whom their white peers regard as "all
right." A white officer might even "59" with one
of these accepted black officers. In general, 59's
and meals are spent with members of the same race.
Some white officers even expressed the view that
they did not feel confident that all black officers
would hurry to assist them in a signal 63 (officer
in trouble). Since a distress call is a symbol for
the necessary unity of police officers, it is dis-
turbing to many that this solidarity, which is so
closely intertwined with the survival and safety of
police officers, has become eroded in recent years.
Several whites openly stated that they would not
back up certain black officers for whom they had a
particular antipathy. Thus, the esprit de corps,
vitally essential to survival, may be threatened by
racial integration.

The sense of trust, so dominant in recollections of the past, is not only dissipated by the
racial and sexual conflict; officers feel that any
other officer might inform on them in order to get
ahead in a department where white upward mobility
is difficult. Two white detectives were sleeping
in their car in the early morning hours, a not uncommon practice. A white, uniformed, morning watch
officer told his superior officer. Both detectives
were punished by suspension and changed to different
shifts. One had been going to school during the
day; the other ran a business. The watch change
disrupted their plans and life-styles. Officers
thus believe that the code of camaraderie is broken.
They also no longer feel support from superior
officers. Black superiors are generally not trusted
at all. White superiors' support is weak due to

their fear of demotion or transfer to a "garbage" assignment. Officers are well aware that their superior officers must placate the ruling hierarchy if they wish to remain sergeants and lieutenants.

A sergeant with nineteen years of experience with the department summed up the way policing used to be and the way it is now:

"Before, I used to enjoy policing very much. I worked six days a week and didn't want a day off. It is distasteful to me now. Things have changed. The courts made some drastic changes that affected police procedure. Racial composition of the department changed. The promotions have gone to incompetents. There's been a change in society's attitude toward police which is understandable because there are a lot of duds in the police department now. It's not any fun anymore. For instance, I see punks on the side of the road but I can't do anything with them now."

It is apparent that many organizational and attitudinal changes have taken place in the last thirty years. The department has nearly tripled in size; the detective bureau has been specialized into squads; the city has been divided into zones with individual radio frequencies; much of the equipment has been mechanized or computerized; blacks and females have become important segments of the whole; police procedure has been radically changed due to judicial decisions; and accompanying all of the changes has been an erosion of the previous trust and camaraderie that was a part of being a member of the police force. As the subsequent chapters will show, the police officer in Atlanta today neither behaves with nor feels the dedication toward his or her job that is glorified in stories of the past and described in previous literature.

Thus, the Atlanta Police Department is a

unique setting for examining the alienation and
cynicism of police officers that have been described for departments without this marked political
factionalism and the extremely low morale of white
officers. The latter may be due to a decrease in
the officers' discretionary power. Police discretion has been described in many studies (Banton
1964; Goldstein 1960; LaFave 1969; Niederhoffer
1969; Skolnick 1967; Westley 1969). The constraints
upon the Atlanta police officers' use of discretion
applied by legal and departmental decisions may contribute to their feelings of frustration.

The department has been a dynamic organization
throughout the last thirty years; often the structural and procedural modifications have been a
reflection of the leadership at the time. Changes
continue to occur as portrayed in Figure 4, which
represents the Atlanta Bureau in 1977.

The commissioner introduced these organizational regroupings without any explanation. One
officer expressed the view that this modified
structure gives the commissioner more direct lines
of influence to more divisions within the Bureau.
It should also be noted that the ex chief, Inman,
now directly oversees Community Relations and THOR.
The chart is reproduced here to illustrate that this
study must be looked at as a view of the Atlanta
Police Department at one point in time. Several
years from now, an observer may well find an
entirely different organization under an entirely
new leadership.

Revised Organization Plan

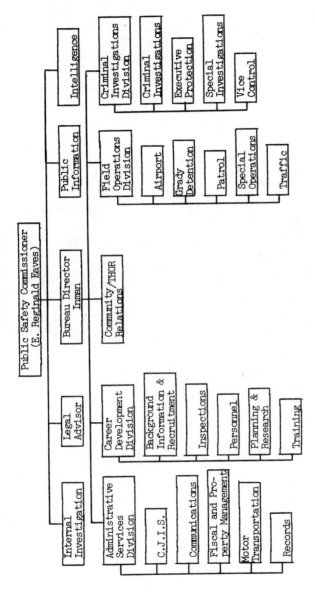

Figure 4

4

DETECTIVES' POLICING ACTIVITIES

This chapter focuses upon the police work performed by several detective squads. The log style presentation will indicate that many hours of the watch, perhaps even the entire shift, may be spent involved in nonregulation activities which are described in Chapter 6. The main purpose of this chapter is to present some of the cases that the detectives work on in order to further illuminate the environment (people and places) that the officers encounter daily. The description is mainly of male police officers since there are few women in detective squads. Two of the four squads (Homicide and Robbery) described in this chapter were all male. As females' tenure in the department increases, more women will advance to the detective rank, and undoubtedly all detective squads will be sexually heterogeneous in the future.

Most detectives work with partners. The sergeant or lieutenant usually assigns a detective's original partnership, but in time an individual may seek a new partner with whom (s)he feels more at ease. There is no interracial partnership at the present time. Since off-days may not coincide, the two-man unit may only function for three or four days of the week. Many officers equate the relationship of detective partners to a marriage, except that most feel closer and talk more to their partners than to their wives. Two officers who have been partners for a length of time do emanate an aura of warmth and deep camaraderie. They are not only workers who share the same case load, but they are also fellow conspirators in breaking the rules, often covering up and protecting each other in turn.

Prior to looking at the activities of several specific squads, let us review the outlined functions of the detectives; instead of the theory, let us examine the actual practices.since there is quite a gap between the ideal and real levels of police performance. The primary function of the detective is to respond to radio requests for his or her particular squad's services. Each detective has a radio number, but if, for example, a homicide occurs and radio requests a homicide detective, the dispatcher does not call a particular detective but says, "Is there a Homicide car on the air?" In theory, every Homicide detective should rush to his microphone and respond, "4172, go ahead." In reality, there is often a pregnant pause which typifies the waiting game--waiting for another Homicide car to answer the call. The dispatcher may in fact have to repeat his question until finally a Homicide detective answers. There is a tacit understanding that one unit does not assume the entire burden of the squad. But there is also a definite lack of enthusiasm and few "gung-ho" detectives.

Arriving at their squad office, detectives check their mailboxes for reports that have been assigned to them for clear-up--their second work function. All reports are supposed to be taken from victims and given complaint numbers. In the past, officers had more discretion and often did not write up or file reports from victims that the officers felt lacked credibility. Today, the detective, faced with the task of clearing up all reports, may resort to several methods. One practice that is wholly against departmental regulations, is to leave the report in one's notebook. At present, as stated above, this act of discretion involves more risk since the hierarchy does not condone it.

If the report is given a complaint number and must be handled in some way, it may be cleared by arrest; or by an "exceptional" label, in which case the name of a perpetrator is given on the report but the victim chooses not to prosecute. Detectives are reputed to employ fictive names and addresses in order to clear a report as "exceptional." This accounts for a high percentage of the aggravated assault clear ups. A report can also be labeled as "no crime" or "unfounded" when either the victim cannot be located or the address on the original report proves to be non-existent.

As it will become apparent from the activities described below, there are few cases in which investigative techniques can be used productively in clearing the reports. Therefore, many detectives visit or telephone the victim on an assigned report and their work on that case ends. Homicide is perhaps the only crime that has to be cleared legitimately or left uncleared.

The third outlined police activity for detectives is to patrol the streets in unmarked cars that theoretically are not known as police cars to the public. The detectives adamantly believe that their Plymouths are well known to criminals and therefore cannot function surreptitiously, only preventively. Detectives' present low morale discourages patrolling, and superior officers cannot effectively oversee the detectives' beat which includes the entire city of Atlanta. Other deterrents to cruising the streets are the condition of the automobiles and the auto insurance controversy. Although the cars are at most three years old, they are continually breaking down and in need of maintenance. Detectives are fond of saying that their cars' "get up and go" got up and left. Therefore, many officers do not feel that their vehicles are in adequate condition to pursue suspicious persons or traffic violators. Lastly, police officers in Atlanta must insure themselves on their personal policies for automobile insurance on vehicles owned by the city. Many officers do not want to expose their vehicles to the risks involved in active police patrolling since they must pay the insurance premiums.

Sex Crimes

Until several years ago crimes presently handled by the Sex Crimes squad fell under the Homicide squad's jurisdiction. A Law Enforcement Assistance Association grant financed the creation of a squad to exclusively handle sex-related crimes. The grant contained several provisos to be employed in the composition of the squad: a certain number of blacks and females were to be included. This prerequisite excluded several white males with years of experience

53

from assignment in the new unit. Also, instead of two-man cars, the operant unit was to be a three-person team integrated racially and sexually. After several months with interracial units, racial conflict surfaced, and the black officers insisted upon segregated cars. Thus, in October 1975, the squad was separated into the following units:

Day Watch (2 cars)		Evening Watch (1 car)	Morning Watch (1 car)
A.	**B.**		
White male	Black male	Black male	White male
White female	Black female	Black female	White male
White female		Black female	White female

Off days were arranged in such a way that all three members of the unit were present on only one watch per week.

The Sex Crimes office is not located in the downtown police station. The rationale for separating this squad is to provide a pleasant environment for rape victims away from the rather sterile and crowded area of the police headquarters. This reasoning, however benevolent in intent, is fallacious since victims are seldom brought to the Sex Crimes office. Reports are generally taken either at the crime scene or en route to Grady Hospital where all victims have to be transported for physical examinations and counseling. The detective unit is often called back to the hospital in order to drive the victim home.

Day Watch:

October 1 (white male and white female detectives)[1]--There were no calls for a Sex Crimes car.

---

[1] The term "detective" used within this chapter includes plainclothes officers. All female officers referred to within this chapter were in fact plainclothes officers.

Worked on one assigned case by riding the rape victim (black female) from the previous night around in attempt to establish the venue of the crime. Detectives had earlier expressed the hope that it would be outside of their jurisdiction. The victim was unable to find the location of the rape. Police work took approximately 45 mintues.

October 2 (two white female detectives)--No calls and no investigative work.

October 3 (two white female detectives)--No calls and no investigative work.

October 7 (white male and white female detectives)--First visited the grandfather of a child molestation victim. He would not speak with females present. The eight-year-old boy was paid several times to allow a middle-aged white male to sodomize him. Later in the watch, the unit returned to interview the victim who used very graphic language to describe the sex acts that he had been involved in. His language sharply conflicted with his young cherubic appearance. The first visit took approximately 15 minutes; the second involved more time (45 minutes) since the victim directed the detectives to the crime locations.

Received a signal 49 (rape). The victim, a white female, age eighteen, was at a zone headquarters to which she had walked. She asserted that the assault had occurred in the car of a white male who had picked her up during her hitchhiking trek from Alabama. Both detectives separately expressed the view that the case was a "hmmy," a broad term applied to most of the cases which implies that either the victim is lying or that due to the circumstances of the case (e.g.hitchhiking) the perpetrator would not be found guilty or even bound over to criminal court. The call took about an hour and a half since the victim was taken to the Rape Crisis Center in Grady Hospital by the detectives.

October 8 (white male, white female)--No calls and no investigative work.

October 9 (two white females)--No calls.
Visited the mother and family friend of a black rape
victim. The detectives were assigned this case and
stated that they were performing their P.R. (Public
Relations) visit in order to show the victim that
the case was still active. The visit consumed only
ten minutes of the watch.

October 10 (two white females)--Received a
child molestation call from a grade school in a white
lower-class neighborhood. Detectives interviewed the
four female complainants whom the officers later described as "rednecks." The four girls were unkempt,
with rotten teeth and body odor. It was determined
that they had been chased by a white middle-aged
male. The call took approximately one hour.

October 11 (white male, white female)--Received
a signal 49. Victim was an intoxicated black female.
who was garrulous and incoherent. Officers felt that
this was a case that fell beneath the "hmmy" status.
They took the report as a matter of regulation but
stated that several months ago, they would have exercised discretion and would not have bothered to write
the case up. Their lieutenant had been enforcing the
rule that reports must be taken from all victims.
The case involved less time than usual (30 minutes)
since the report was hurriedly written en route to
Grady Hospital.

Evening Watch:

October 15 (black male)--No calls received.
Visited an alleged black rape victim who claimed to
have found a threatening note in her mailbox. The
visit took about 30 minutes; it was prolonged by the
victim's husband who posed many questions to the
detective. The detective felt that she had been
playing around on her husband and had fabricated a
rape story after the husband had beaten her up. In
a later conversation, the day watch detective who
had originally taken the report expressed an identi-
cal view of the case.

October 16 (black male, black female)--Received

a call to Grady Hospital to interview the parents of
a child molestation victim, a two-year-old black
child who had been sodomized. The officers felt that
with the child's inability to express the details of
the crime, there was little chance of catching the
perpetrator. It should be noted at this point that
crimes that involve children as victims are almost
the only type of case that evokes an emotional
response from the police officers. The call took
about 20 minutes, the length of time required to
elicit data for the report from the mother and aunt
of the victim.

Received a signal 49, an attempted rape on a
thirteen-year-old black girl. During the initial
interview between the victim and the female detective (the male detective was outside guarding the
perpetrator) the victim stated that she had volun-
tarily entered the apartment of the eighteen-year-
old male. She further stated that no penetration
had occurred. The girl's version of the incident
was entirely different the next day in city court.
She now claimed both coersion and penetration. The
perpetrator was bound over without bond. Two weeks
later, aided by the detective's statement concerning
the victim's initial account of the incident, he was
not indicted by the grand jury. The interviews,
arrest, and booking consumed over two hours of the
watch. Although the perpetrator was transported to
the city jail by a uniform car, the detective unit
also had to be present at the booking.

October 17 (black male, two black females)--
Went to municipal court at four o'clock for the preliminary hearing of yesterday's attempted rape.
Afterward, the detectives spent two hours at the
station taking the statements of the victim, perpetrator, and the two girl friends of the victim who
were acting as witnesses. The detectives also had
to write up supplementary reports for the district
attorney to present to the grand jury. This amount
of time spent on paper work is not unusual. Any
case that is cleared by arrest involves a great number of reports, statements, and forms.

After leaving the downtown station, the male detective who was driving (with any sexually heterogeneous unit, the male always drives) spotted a driver who appeared to be "under the influence." The detective car began to follow the suspect and called for a uniform car to intercept the DUI. The suspect speeded up and a chase commenced, culminating in an accident involving the suspect's car and a truck. This episode was the only incident observed in which detectives involved themselves in a pursuit activity that was not a matter of rules but of initiative. The incident took approximately 40 minutes.

A signal 49 was received. The case was a day old and therefore the victim, a fourteen-year-old black girl, was not taken to Grady Hospital for physical examination. The officers were sympathetic to the girl but all three later expressed skepticism and labeled it as a "hmmy." Little time was alloted to the call; about 20 minutes to write the report.

October 18 (two black females)--Received one signal 49. Detectives again felt that the case was a "hmmy." The white female victim had separated from her husband two days previously. She asserted that the day before, two males had knocked at her door; she had let them in and they had raped her. There were some definite inconsistencies in her story which the estranged husband, who was present at the interview, pointed out. The detectives did not question the victim's statement but merely took the report and called radio for a complaint number. The case took about an hour; although the victim was not taken to the Rape Crisis Center, the interview was interrupted several times by the arrival and subsequent garrulousness of an inebriated neighbor.

Following normal procedure, the detectives handed the report into the station. The next day, it was returned to the Sex Crimes sergeant who assigned it to a day watch team since day watch receives fewer calls. The day watch unit, in this case, made a P.R. visit to the victim and the case ended--uncleared. The Day Watch detectives also

58

expressed disbelief about the woman's allegations and indicated their belief that she was an alcoholic.

October 20 (black female)--No calls and no investigative work.

Morning Watch:

October 22 (two white males)--No calls but the unit was active in what the detectives termed "anti-rape" work. This involved checking abandoned buildings which are frequent locations of rape. The unit also drove around to previous rape crime scenes often leaving the car and scanning the area with flashlights. This surveillance activity was performed throughout the watch and took approximately four hours. This unusual length of time spent on police work may be ascribed to the adventuresome aspect of the activities which were accompanied by much joking and personal conversation.

October 23 (two white males)--Two signal 49's were received during the watch. The detectives labeled both cases as "hmmys." The first involved an intoxicated black female who claimed to have been kidnapped and raped. She had been walking in a "bar and club" area at three o'clock in the morning. This call consumed about 30 minutes since the detectives escorted the victim to the hospital.

The second report was taken from a white female in a "hippie" apartment which was extremely dirty and overridden with bugs. This type of apartment is the norm to date. The victim claimed that she and her boyfriend had fought and he had left the apartment, leaving the door unlocked. She alleged that shortly after his departure a white male entered and raped her. The ID unit was called. This call took almost 70 minutes since the detectives waited until the ID unit had completed its tasks. It might also be noted that the victim was quite attractive which may have prolonged the male detectives' stay.

The detectives also went from bar to bar searching for a particular informant. They finally located him on a street corner and became involved

in a heated discussion which included the use of
their slapjacks. The search and subsequent "interview" took approximately two hours since the detectives often lingered in the bars.

October 24 (two white males, one white female)--Received one signal 49. As usual, the
female detective wrote up the report. This was a
statistically unusual case since it involved a
black female victim and a white male perpetrator.
The victim had taken a walk in the middle of the
night to "get a coca-cola." The three detectives
privately labeled the case as a "hmmy" since they
felt she had set herself up and could not identify
her attacker. The call consumed about 30 minutes.

October 25 (white male, white female)--The
first call of the watch was an attempted rape that
was mentioned in Chapter 2--the Crime Prevention
unit had installed new locks that day. The white
female victim had left her patio door wide open,
and a white male entered the apartment and attempted
to rape her. Her apartment was also indescribably
filthy with cockroaches everywhere. The condition
of the complainant's home seemed to have an effect
upon the attitude of the police officers who were
noticeably cold and aloof. The ID unit was called
and the case took approximately 90 minutes. The
victim was unusually hysterical (to date victims
were quite calm if sober) and detectives remained
with her until her boyfriend arrived.

The second call was to the downtown bus station
where a black female, waiting for a bus to Alabama,
claimed to have been abducted and raped. The officers felt that she was shading the truth and had
probably entered the car willingly. It is exactly
this type of case, the questionable circumstances
and truthfulness of the victim, which constitutes a
"hmmy." The female officer took both reports. This
call took more than an hour since the detectives
drove the victim to several parking lots in an
attempt to establish the exact location and, possibly, the perpetrator's vehicle. The case proved
to be unusual since the suspect was in fact arrested
that night. However, his arrest was by a uniformed

officer who had apprehended him for robbery.

October 26 (white male, white female)--No calls and no investigative work.

October 28 (two white males)--Very busy night. The first call was to a housing project and involved a sixty-nine-year-old white female known to the police officers as a "24" (demented person). She claimed that two black males and one black female entered her apartment through a window. The former allegedly both raped her while the girl watched. The ID unit was called and the victim transported to Grady. The call involved nearly an hour of the watch since the victim insisted both upon giving an extremely detailed account of the incident and upon showing the officers the various parts of her home which the alleged rapists had touched. The detectives made numerous humorous references to the case during the rest of the watch.

The next report involved a seventeen-year-old who had been forced into a car by a black male. This case was also labeled a "hmmy" since the victim could not identify the type of car or the face of the perpetrator. Thus, there was actually no possibility of arresting him. Nevertheless, the unit took the victim to the crime scene, a heavily wooded area, and spent nearly an hour futilely searching for a prophylactic that the perpetrator had used. The rationale for this search was not verbalized and, ironically, it was the closest thing to actual investigative legwork done by detectives this month.

The next two signal 49's both involved twenty-two-year-old women. The first victim was extremely intoxicated and hysterical. The report was taken quickly and the woman transported to Grady (15 minutes).

In the next case, the victim was white and lived in an affluent area of the city (both facts unusual thus far). She stated that upon getting out of her car at four o'clock in the morning at her home, she was jumped and raped. The officers were unusually solicitous and courteous, perhaps due to her race and socioeconomic level. After escorting her to the hospital, however, they discussed the case and agreed that there had been flaws in her story and that it was in fact a "hmmy." Both officers also were convinced that she was a police groupie since she had mentioned knowing several specific Atlanta police officers. This call took almost one hour since the detectives became involved in social conversation with the victim.

October 29 (two white males)--Handled one signal 49 with a white female victim who at first appeared to the detectives to be a "genuine rape" victim. In the course of taking the report the fact surfaced that the victim willingly entered the perpetrator's car and had in fact driven around with him for several hours prior to the rape. The police officers labeled the victim as the "Amazon" due to her girth and joked about the case for the duration of the watch. The call involved almost an hour and a half since the victim was driven around the area by the detectives in an attempt to establish venue.

October 30 (two white males, one white female)--No calls received. Detectives decided to search for a certain prostitute informant. This not only entailed several hours standing around strip clubs and topless bars, but also involved going to several motels that cater to prostitutes, banging on doors, and chasing several persons. The hunt was unsuccessful and the rationale behind it unclear. It easily consumed three hours of the shift.

Morning watch personnel are notorious for doing rather crazy things in order to produce some excitement. The few irregular activities mentioned in this chapter stand out as those which presumably involved law enforcement. Most of the illegal and irregular activities are practiced without even attempting to explain them with a policing rationale.

October 31 (two white males, 1 white female)--Had one call which impressed the unit as a "good" rape. The victim was a middle-aged white female

whose middle-class home had been broken into by a
white male who had then raped her. The female officer who had interviewed the victim alone later commented that she doubted if the woman would prosecute. She had unwillingly called the police under
pressure from a neighbor. Her husband was out of
town, and she did not want him to know that the
assault had occurred. It is therefore ironic that
in the one case of the entire month that the detectives felt would hold up in court, the victim would
not in all probability even prosecute. The case
took about one hour.

Having surveyed one month of police activity of
the Sex Crimes squad, several strong impressions
stand out. The cynicism of the officers seems to be
reinforced by the type of victim they encounter.
The usual rape victim has, the officers believe,
been forcibly assaulted. But she has usually placed
herself in what the officers believe to be a compro-
mising position, such as hitchhiking or taking midnight walks in a high crime area. Only token investigation is undertaken since the officers either do
not believe that the case will hold up in court or
that the victim will testify or cooperate. The
usual victim also comes from a lower-class background. Both her home and personal hygiene may not
be in accordance with the values of the police
officers.

The detectives employ much discretion in their
encounters with the victims--in their attitude
toward them, in the content of their reports, and
in their presentations to the grand jury. Overtly
sympathetic to most victims, both male and female
officers often later joke about them and the circumstances that had led to the assaults. Frequently,
the female partner(s) are even more skeptical than
their male colleagues. In the two sexually mixed
units observed, when partnered with a male, the
female officer never drove and almost always did the
paper work. On the male officer's days off, the two
women often went home, did no investigative work,
and avoided any police-related topic of conversation.

Homicide

The Homicide squad personnel divide the homicide cases they work on into three groups: (1) domestic, in which victim and perpetrator know each other, versus nondomestic, or stranger-to-stranger; (2) alcohol-precipitated versus nonalcohol-related; and (3) spontaneous versus premeditated. Most of the homicides and aggravated assaults that the squad handles are domestic, alcohol-precipitated, and spontaneous. Therefore, the perpetrator is usually known and acknowledges his guilt. There are few "who-dun-its."

There were no females working on the Homicide squad during the observation period. The explanation offered by males for the absence of women was that no female has enough police experience to qualify for homicide detection which is presumed to necessitate a certain police acumen acquired by years of police work. However, there were males working on the squad who did not have years of experience. Throughout the department, this is considered an elite squad to which many detectives aspire.

A homicide detective has to be called to the scene of a homicide, suicide, or natural death (at home) by the Uniform division. Homicide detectives are not usually called to the scenes of aggravated assaults; instead, the uniformed officer takes the report which then follows the route from Report Review to the Homicide watch sergeant who assigns the case to a detective.

Day Watch:

<u>November 3</u> (white male)--Received one call, a double murder and suicide. A black male had shot his two-month-old son, his four-year-old stepdaughter, and himself. The bodies were not at the crime scene when the Homicide unit arrived. They had been transported to Grady Hospital for emergency care. All three died.

The apartment was in a government housing project but was cleaner and tidier than the average.

A large puddle of blood slowly coagulated on the living-room floor. A bottle of juice and an infant seat were grim reminders of the young children who had been killed. Upstairs, there was another pool of blood on the bed where the infant had been sleeping when shot. The call took almost two hours. The initial 45 minutes was spent locating the address. Although the detective had responded first to radio's request for a Homicide unit, three other Homicide cars (including the lieutenant) arrived at the scene some minutes prior to the detective.

The motive for the crime was unclear. The homicide officers often call domestic homicides "chicken bone" or "neckbone killings," an allusion to several killings that stemmed from arguments over who was to eat which part of the chicken. The white officers who have worked in Homicide for any length of time freely express their belief that the lower-class blacks in Atlanta use violence in situations where the white population would use words. Thus, it is not uncommon for detectives to describe the housing projects as a zoo. When a killing occurs there, the usual white police reaction is, "The animals have been fighting again." Violence is so common in the projects that killings do not appear to cause the shock and alarm that they do in other areas of the city. One does not see a crowd of shocked people in the project; if the people gather, it is an informal and often joking type of group.

November 4 (white male)--Most of the day was spent in the investigation of the murder/rape of a female "wino" that had occurred several days previously. The crime scene was the back-yard area of an abandoned building in the wino district. Blood stains were still visible on the brick wall. The detective drove around the area, stopping frequently to question the clusters of drunks in the area. One old man was brought to the car and questioned, but little information could be gleaned from his incoherent responses. Later, the officer joked about having the car fumigated and deodorized. The detective also went around to several rather seedy hotels searching for a possible lead. The officer explained that normally with a "wino" murder little investiga-

tive work was done. This particular case, gruesome
and sordid enough to engender much publicity, had
led the commissioner to apply pressure to the
squad's lieutenant to make at least token gestures
of investigation. The investigative activities
took approximately two hours.

The detective also spent several hours in an
assistant district attorney's office in order to
review his testimony in an impending homicide trial.

November 7 (white male)--Continued the investigation of the "wino" murder by visiting the mother
and sister of the victim who lived in a housing project. Visit took about 20 minutes.

Received a signal 48 (dead person) to a black
housing project. Found a seven-week-old baby dead
in a crib amid garbage and dirty laundry. The detective remained at the scene until the medical examiner
arrived and briefly examined the infant. His tenta-
tive diagnosis of cause of death was natural crib
death. The detective was skeptical since a baby of
that age can be suffocated without any visible signs,
such as bruises, appearing. Several neighbors later
called the Homicide office and volunteered information concerning previous abuse to the deceased
infant's older siblings (e.g. setting a child on the
heated burner of a stove). However, no investigation took place and the case was closed as a natural
death.

It should be noted that none of the officers
present at the scene were visibly affected by either
the dead infant or the environment of the home. The
detective said that he had seen it so many times that
it has ceased to affect him. He spent about 45 mintues on the call; the medical examiner's arrival was
more prompt than usual.

November 8 (two white males)--Received a signal
50 (shooting) to Grady Hospital. A black male had
been shot in the head by a "friend" during a heated
discussion. As the detectives attempted to fill out
the "Crime Against Persons" report, the victim
stated that he did not want to prosecute. "I am a

66

Negro and will handle it that way, and take care of it." The detectives concluded the incident by charging the "victim" with simple battery and the "perpetrator" was charged with aggravated assault. The officers felt that both cases would be dismissed in municipal court--as they proved to be. The detectives were pulled out on the call for about 40 minutes (unavailable for other duties); however, most of that time was spent socializing with the uniformed officers assigned to detention.

November 9 (white male)--Spent the morning (two hours) in the Homicide office "clearing" aggravated assault reports. Issued one warrant on a black male in a project whom a neighbor accused of assault.

November 10 (white male)--Spent several hours clearing reports. Issued and served one warrant on a black male accused of assaulting his estranged wife. The recipient of the warrant was cordial and agreeable in conversation with the detective. The latter exercised his discretion and issued him a copy of arrest charges, instead of taking him to jail. The copy of charges dictates that the accused appear in city court on a certain date, in this particular case, the next day.

November 11 (two white males)--Received a signal 48. Neighbors had discovered the body of a middle-aged black male. Death had apparently occurred several days previously since the body showed signs of decomposition. An overpowering stench filled the two-room shack, caused by the body and the condition of the house. The detective searched the room for medication or signs of foul play. The only object of interest to the detective was a bottle of shaving lotion which persuaded him that the deceased was probably a wino since that particular lotion has a fairly potent alcohol content and is frequently purchased by winos. The medical examiner was called and the death was labeled a natural. The call took about one hour.

In municipal court the detective became uncharacteristically upset when he spotted the man whom he had given a copy of charges the day before in the prisoners' section under armed guard. Apparently the perpetrator had gone to his ex-wife's home the previous night and attempted to kill her. She had shot at him six times. The officer was depressed and said, "See, this is what happens when you try to be a nice guy."

November 14 (white male)--Went to city court on a domestic aggravated assault report. The husband in the case was bound over on $2,000 bail. Another assault between the couple and the witnesses almost occurred in court as everyone shouted accusations at each other. The detective said that this was typical for city court or "city circus." No other calls or investigations occurred during the watch.

November 15 (white male)--No homicide calls or investigations. Everyone in the office has been talking about the unusually slow homicide rate this month.

Evening Watch:

November 16 (white male)--The detective first went to Grady Hospital to interview a stabbing victim--a sixty-nine-year-old black male who had been stabbed in the heart by his sixty-eight-year-old wife. The aged victim stated that he had been stabbed by her three or four times in the past after both got "liquored up." Once again, a homicide detective commented upon the acceptance of physical violence within the black lower-class community. The detective spent approximately 15 minutes talking to the victim.

Later in the evening, the detective chose to relax at the city morgue, his favorite crack.[2] The

---

[2]Crack is a term that will be fully discussed in Chapter 6. Used either as a verb or as a noun, it means a place to relax or sleep, away from the eyes of superior officers and the public.

Atlanta morgue does not cover the bodies nor are they placed in drawers. The deceased are placed nude on metal tables. On this particular evening, there were two black male corpses. One was a victim of a homicide that had occurred on day watch; the other was a "natural" who had already had an autopsy as evidenced by the large T-shaped incision across the chest and down the abdomen. The morgue is a popular spot to take observers and other civilian personnel. The officers, hardened to the sight of death from repeated exposure to it, enjoy watching the reaction of non-police.

November 17 (white male)--Received one call which radio labeled as a kidnapping. It turned out to be a domestic incident involving a father who had taken his child from the legal custody of the mother. A Community Relations car was called to handle the situation. The detective spent about 30 minutes on the call since the rather hysterical complainant requested that he remain with her until the arrival of the Community Relations officer.

November 18 (white male)--Received no calls and no clear-ups handled.

November 20 (white male)--Received two signal 53's (suicides). The first call was to a bar where a white male (age twenty-five) had shot himself in the head while sitting alone in a booth. Since it was a suicide, the medical examiner handled the case. The detective did interview several witnesses to the shooting and ascertained that the victim had been depressed concerning his estrangement from his wife. The call took approximately one hour.

The other suicide involved the eighteen-year-old son of a very prominent white Atlanta physician. Upon arriving at the scene, the detective immediately observed the body of the deceased being lifted into a hearse. This action was against all city regulations which the detective felt a doctor would be cognizant of. The boy's room was searched by the officer. The medical examiner took over the case upon his arrival and tentatively diagnosed the cause of death as a drug overdose. The atmosphere in the

69

house was strangely muted and nongrieving in comparison to the other crime scenes. The detective expressed his feeling that something was not "kosher" in the case but the medical examiner's verdict was not questioned and the case was over. The detective only spent about 20 minutes on this call since it seemed apparent that police presence was not desired.

November 21 (two black males)--No calls or clear-up investigation.

November 22 (white male)--No calls and no clear-up investigation.

Morning Watch:

November 24 (two white males)--No calls or investigations.

November 25 (two white males)--Received one call, signal 50 (shooting) to Grady Hospital where the participants had been taken by uniformed officers. Three people were involved in the episode, but all were antagonistic to the police and would not talk. The detectives felt sure that no prosecution would take place. They only spent about ten minutes interviewing the men but remained at the hospital for almost an hour talking to other police officers.

November 26 (white male sergeant)--No calls. The detectives handled the paper work in the office, mainly reading over aggravated assault reports and assigning them to the individual detectives. No cases are assigned to the morning watch detectives for post investigative work since victims and witnesses are not readily available for interviews in the middle of the night.

November 27 (white male)--Assisted another car of detectives as they staked out a gas station awaiting the return of a man who had allegedly asked another man to commit a murder for him. After an hour the detectives decided that it had probably only been a joke and they left the area.

As stated earlier, November 1975 was a particularly slow month for Homicide in Atlanta. The few
cases do indicate a degree of coldness, even callous-
ness, toward the gore and death that are encountered
by the officers. One of the squad's favorite activities is to show civilian observers photographs of
certain deaths where victims were decapitated or shot
with high-power shotguns at extremely close range.
War stories often describe the blood, guts, and
stench of various homicides witnessed. This almost
macabre behavior seems to be a necessary part of an
occupation in which the human "sensibilities" are
attacked constantly by the sight of violent death.

The atmosphere of the sexually homogeneous squad
differs markedly from the Sex Crimes unit. The mood
is more like that of a men's club, with talk centering on sex, women, sex, sports, and sex. Sexual
joking and innuendos towards the female observer and
female officers were commonplace.

Robbery

Robbery was also an all-male detective squad.
In December 1975, the age range of the squad was
broader than that of the other squads discussed with
several detectives in their forties and fifties.
The squad works on rotating shifts that change every
six weeks. Until recently, however, the two morning
watch detectives were permanently assigned to that
watch.

All Robbery detectives have partners.[3] Most of
the partner relationships, both at work and in leisure
hours, have been long term and appear to produce
strong relationships. The Robbery squad is inundated
with reports of purse-snatching and pickpocketing.

----

[3]One detective was working alone during evening
watch since his partner had been moved to day watch.
For several weeks therefore, I was able to ride with
him and function as a pseudopartner.

Usually the only description of the assailant is "black male with an afro." Thus, there is actually little investigation possible.

Day Watch:

December 1 (two white males)--One signal 44 (robbery) which both detectives felt was a "hmmy." A man who did clean-up work at night in a restaurant claimed to have been kidnapped while working, driven around for several hours during the night, and robbed of $100. Upon questioning, certain facts which the officers considered relevant came to light. The victim owed his employer $100 and was several months behind in his car payments. The detectives were overtly sympathetic and polite, but later, in the car, they discussed the transparency of the "victim's" motivation in fabricating a tale of robbery. The call took almost one and a half hours since the victim was interviewed several times.

December 2 (two white males)--No robbery calls occurred during the watch. Apparently, this is not unusual since Robbery detectives are not always called when a robbery occurs. The uniformed officer may write the report which eventually is given to a Robbery detective to investigate. The Uniform division only calls for a detective if the perpetrator is being held or if there are any unusual circumstances concerning the case.

The detectives worked in coordination with several FBI agents in the attempted apprehension of a man wanted for several robberies and homicides. Guided by an informant, the two cars staked out an apartment building and later entered it. The wanted felon was not there. The entire afternoon (3 hours) was spent with the FBI men; much of the time was spent in the Robbery office awaiting a telephone call from an informant.

December 4 (white male)--No calls or investigative work.

December 5 (white male)--No calls received. Detective went to an assistant district attorney's

72

office in order to review his testimony in a pending bank robbery trial.

December 6 (white male)--No calls. Spent most of the watch in the Robbery office as the detective telephoned victims and witnesses and caught up on his paper work. Two perpetrators, a teenage couple, were brought into the office by a uniformed officer. They were accused of stealing and using credit cards. The girl was surly and defiant, but the detective maintained a polite interrogative posture. Later he did comment that she was badly in need of an "attitude readjustment" program, a term which refers to the police officers' use of slapjacks and other force.

While riding back to the station from lunch, a man waved the detective car down and said that a black male wearing a black hat was at a nearby intersection shooting at passersby. The tension in the car mounted as the detective quickly proceeded to the area. Upon arrival, the anticlimax which is normal in policework occurred since the gunman (real or mythical) had vanished.

Policing is normally unexciting and calm. Then, at a second's notice, something happens--a certain signal on the radio for example, and the calm is abandoned as the adrenalin floods through the police officers. One can feel excitement and tension grow in the car, almost reaching a point that is unbearable in the electricity of the moment. Nine times out of ten it ends anticlimactically, and the mood shoots down to the original calm, or the energy may be used to follow illegal pursuits.

Evening Watch:

December 9 (white male)--One signal 44 was received from a dry cleaning store. The detective later speculated that it may have been an "inside" job since the perpetrator had directed the clerk to remove all cash from a box located in the back of the store. However, no further investigation took place. The incident only involved about 20 minutes, the length of time required to obtain quickly the

73

necessary data for the report.

December 10 (white male)--No calls but en
route to a victim's apartment, the detective's car
broke down. Had to call a tow truck and be pulled
to the police gas and automobile service station
("the shop"). The detective was disgusted and said
it was typical of the poor quality vehicles the
Department supplies.

December 11 (white male)--No calls. Visited
an old couple who lived in a tiny house with almost
every inch filled with furniture, trash, and miscellaneous items. The husband and wife had been
robbed and assaulted. The woman (whom the detective
later described as a probable "24") rambled on and
on while her husband, a mute, kept waving his arms
wildly. The interview took almost an hour, and
although this observer neared a state of suppressed
hysteria, the officer remained calm, smiling and
spoke   sympathetically.

December 12 (two white males)--This was an
eventful night. First, detective radio called for
any car in a certain area to be on the lookout for
a stolen car. The Robbery car was immediately in
the midst of a chase that culminated in the arrest
of the car thieves. Auto theft handled the report.
This incident took over an hour since the Robbery
detectives agreed to remain with the stolen vehicle
until the tow truck arrived to impound it.

Next, a signal 44 came over the radio, accompanied by additional information on the fleeing
perpetrators. The detective car raced to the area.
One officer spotted the two running black males and
the chase was on. By the time the perpetrators were
apprehended, a veritable convention of police officers was taking place--a total of ten Uniform and
Detective cars had arrived at the scene.(a common
occurrence when anything exciting or dangerous "is
going down"). The perpetrators were conveyed to the
Robbery office in a Uniform car since detective cars,
without protective screening, are not ideal for
transporting prisoners. At the office, the paper
work on this case consumed more than two hours, and

the detectives worked one hour beyond the watch change. First, the men arrested had to be read their rights and their waiver of counsel forms. Two arrest forms and a robbery report had to be filled out. The three witnesses' statements had to be taken. The stolen money, mostly coins, had to be counted twice. Then, a line-up was conducted, and finally the perpetrators were taken downstairs for booking. The entire case took up approximately three and a half hours of the shift.

In order to conduct the line-up, one detective went into the city jail, which is on the same floor as the Robbery office, and requested the presence of six black male prisoners, approximately twenty years of age. The eight men were lined up behind a two-way mirror. Their names, dates of birth, height, and weight were then listed on the line-up forms. After the witnesses had observed them and selected those who, in their opinions, were the perpetrators, the line of men was brought out to be photographed by an officer from the ID unit.

December 13 (two black males, one white male)--Called to Underground Atlanta (a major tourist trap according to officers) on a robbery signal. The victim, a middle-aged white male, was intoxicated and behaved in a lewd and boisterous manner. His wife and daughter corroborated his story of having been jostled and pickpocketed by the young black male who was being held by uniformed officers. The call took about two hours since everyone involved was taken to the Robbery office where each was interviewed separately and made formal statements. Two days later, in municipal court, the victim's account differed on many points from his original statement. The perpetrator who proclaimed total innocence, was bound over however.

An older white male detective patrolled a lower class, racially mixed area of Zone 3 known as the Hill District. This was highly unusual since to date few officers have executed preventative patrol duties. He stopped frequently to speak to people standing at street corners and outside of bars. People often waved to him, and he remarked that he knew just about everyone and what they were "up to" from his years as a uniformed officer.

December 15 (two white males)--First went to court on the December 13 Underground Atlanta case. Then, two individuals wanted for several robberies were spotted and apprehended by Uniform. The Robbery detectives arrived at the scene and took the two white perpetrators to the Robbery office. One "snitched" on a third person in order to attain a better bargaining position. He directed the detectives to a stolen car and pointed out the apartment where the perpetrator was staying.

The detectives staked out the car for about two hours hoping that the individual would return to it. They sat in the detective car in the pouring rain discussing only non-police matters such as hunting and sex. It was an easygoing and companionable time. Then they went to the apartment; one stood guard at the back, and the other went in the front. The "pull" (making an arrest) was successful and the perpetrator was taken to the station and booked.

Making a pull is acknowledged as the high-risk aspect of the police work. When a detective is riding without a partner, he will usually call for a Uniform car to back him up. On this occasion, the atmosphere during the stakeout had been casual and sociable. When the time occurred for the pull, however, tension could be felt through the car, and professionalism was reinstated as the "battle" plans were discussed. After the arrest the mood shifted back immediately to easygoing conversation, although now accompanied by a sense of elation and accomplishment. The various activities on this case consumed more than one half of the total watch.

December 16 (white male)--The detective called a Uniform car to meet him (59) to discuss a case the uniformed officer had initially handled. The detective required some additional information concerning the home address of one of the suspects, a black female juvenile.

76

December 17 (white male)--For approximately
15 minutes, visited the family of the missing
juvenile suspect. The mother told the detective
that the fourteen-year-old was living with her boyfriend (the other suspect). Surrounded by four of
her children, the woman expressed deep concern for
her daughter and a desire for her return. The detective later commented on this family describing
it as a "good" black family. The source of his
approval was the fact that the woman held a job and
the family did not live in a housing project.
Wambaugh (1970) commented upon the different reaction of the police officers to blacks who are
employed. "Gus realized that policemen expected so
little of Negroes that a job alone and clean children were unalterable proof that this was a decent
man as opposed to the ones with dirty children who
were probably the enemy" (Wambaugh 1970: 139).

December 18 (two white males)--No calls.
Visited a black male robbery victim who lived in an
extremely lavish and "mod" apartment. Detectives
were overtly sympathetic and polite. After returning to the car, however, they both expressed the
view that the victim was a drug dealer and the robbery had been rooted in the dealing business. The
interview had been for "PR" reasons and took approximately 10 to 15 minutes, the standard amount of
time for a PR visit.

Also went looking for the black male boyfriend
in the December 16 juvenile case. The address given
by the girl's mother was an apartment in a housing
project. It is always difficult to locate the correct building letter and apartment number in projects. After a lengthy search for the apartment,
one detective pounded at the front door shouting
"Police," while his partner stood on the rear stairs
guarding the back door. When the door was opened,
the officer entered gun in hand and explained who he
was searching for. While a small child slept on the
living-room couch, the detectives searched the
dwelling. The suspect was not there, and later
information placed both suspects in Alabama.

This pull was one of the few occasions where

77

the detectives' actions coincided with the popular image of police detective excitement and drama. However, the tense drama of approaching the door and bounding in with weapon in hand was preceded by a half hour of tedious and anticlimactic driving from building to building in the maze of a government housing project. The investigation took approximately one hour.

December 19 (two white males)--One call consumed most of the shift. The signal involved the robbery of a shoe store: Spent a great deal of time searching for the perpetrator. A Uniform car located the perpetrator's vehicle overturned in a deep ravine. The police officers climbed down to the car in order to search it and to find registration information from the identification of the tag. Having obtained the owner's name and address from radio, the next two hours were spent attempting to locate the address. Atlanta is made up of many streets that stop at certain points and then continue several blocks away. Detectives, whose "beats" include the entire city, are not familiar with every area. An inordinate amount of time is therefore spent driving up and down streets, flashing a light at house numbers, in the attempt to find desired addresses. On this particular evening the search proved to be futile since the perpetrator no longer lived at that address.

December 22 (white male)--Detective spent most of the watch in the office talking to FBI agents.

December 23 (white male)--No calls and no investigative work.

December 24 (white male)--No calls and no investigative work.

December 28 - 31 (white male)--No robbery calls on evening watch. Visited several victims for PR.

The Robbery squad differed in some ways from both Sex Crimes and Homicide. In Homicide, an all-

male group, almost every detective was divorced.
Intrasquad solidarity was relatively weak. Talking
in the squad room centered on impersonal topics
such as sports and sex. The Robbery squad was composed of some older men, and most of the group was
married. Conversations were often focused around
wives, children, and houses. Robbery personnel
spent more time in the office combining some police
work (calling victims) with personal talks. The
atmosphere was warm and cohesive, perhaps owing to
the congenial and popular watch sergeants. Thus,
the personalities and behavior of superior officers
appear to affect the atmosphere and morale of a
squad or zone.

Narcotics

The description of the Narcotics squad will
not be presented in a log form. Their system of
operations differs markedly from the detectives' work
pattern elucidated above. Much of the squad's time
is spent in the office contacting informants and
nurturing drug connections. Most of their remaining
police work involves making buys and building up to
the "big bust." At the time of this study, although
fully aware of the large drug syndicates operating
in Atlanta, most the squad's efforts were directed
to the small-time drug dealers. Since the squad's
enforcement territory covers the outlying areas of
Atlanta, many of their activities are performed in
conjunction with Gwinnett, Cobb, and Dekalb Counties
narcotics agents.

Almost all male squad members, except the
superior officers, had long hair, beards, and wore
hippie clothing. The only females in the squad in
July 1976 were two plainclothes officers temporarily
assigned on a new plan to circulate personnel
through the Vice squads on a monthly basis. They
too wore casual clothing in an attempt to emulate
the drug user and buyer. The officers carried their
revolvers in ankle holsters. The beard and the gun
symbolize a rather schizophrenic existence which
some officers say could drive you crazy after awhile.

Drug informants are usually developed through drug arrests. The detectives believe that the average dealer, given a choice between prison or "pimping" on a fellow dealer, will always pimp unless they are too young and naive. Although these snitches are not admired by the officers, the incentives offered by the police are such that the officers feel a dealer would be stupid not to snitch. A second source of informants are family members and "friends" who call Narcotics desiring an end to a dealer's activities. The third type of informant is the paid snitch who is regarded with the least favor by police officers.

It is the informants who provide the necessary impetus for the squad's effective functioning. Thus, when an officer is transferred from Narcotics, he bequeathes his informants to his replacement. Officers newly assigned to Narcotics are also taught necessary drug information and jargon. One must learn the terms for quantities of every drug and their street values. Two sets of terms are learned, since blacks have different nicknames for most of the drugs, e.g., heroine is referred to as "boy" among blacks, and cocaine is called "girl."

Within the squad, there was one exception to the general description and work pattern of a Narcotics detective. This officer, older than the others, dressed more conventionally, was smooth shaven with shorter hair. He expressed a lack of interest in busting the small-time dealers since he was convinced that a black syndicate, made up of several big-time dealers, was forming a massive drug operation in Atlanta that could extend throughout the Southeast. He had persuaded the lieutenant to allow him to work only on this investigation. The tactics he employed strongly deviated from the romantic, daring exploits depicted in television and the theater. Day after day he rode past the homes and legitimate businesses of the known dealers--his main purpose, to record the license plate numbers of automobiles; check them through NCIC (National Crime Information Center); and perhaps establish a pattern of interaction between the dealers and others. The secondary aim of the daily patrol was harassment.

Not at all surreptitious in his movements, the detective hoped to make the dealers nervous and in some way disrupt their operations. He also utilized informants who unfortunately could only give hints of the magnitude of the transactions involved since they were only on the periphery of the syndicate. His third prong of investigation involved meetings with federal law enforcement agents in which they pooled information concerning the individual operators. This detective's work was solitary and tedious, but he stands out as one of the few white Atlanta police officers who feels a dedication and motivation for his job. It is ironic that he largely created the assignment himself.

As stated above, most Narcotics officers are assigned to making drug buys and busting drug dealers. The typical drug buy, known as the "buy and ride," involves the employment of at least three detectives. One officer is the undercover buyer. His car is backed up by two or more undercover cars that park within sight of the drug transaction. These automobiles purchased for Narcotics are a source of ridicule among the squad members. Although the purpose of a backup car is to remain unobtrusive, one of the cars is a red Barracuda. According to the detectives, there are only two or three red Barracudas in the entire city.

At the buy scene the backup units separate. If the buy is in an apartment complex, one car will park in the same driveway as the buyer while the other watches from the next driveway.[4] The buyer will attempt to complete the transaction out of doors within the eyesight of his "partners." However, the agent is often forced to go inside a house or apartment. The backup cars must wait until he returns to the car. Some officers have reputations

_____

[4]Coincidentally, the first buy and ride that I observed occurred in my own complex, in Dekalb County outside of Atlanta. Seated in backup unit 2, I was amazed when we parked directly in front of my own apartment.

for spending several hours indoors during a buy, sitting and socializing with the dealer while two or three detectives sit in their cars slandering him and their job. After the buy is made, the cars meet several blocks away to discuss the details of the transaction. The drugs are subsequently turned into the state lab for analysis. The findings frequently contradict the dealer's assertions of drug content. Several "buy and rides" may be made from a dealer prior to the bust.

There are two main types of drug busts. The first is an arrest on a warrant which generally involves the procedures enacted in the following case.

One evening, the target of a warrant bust was an apartment in a housing project. The warrant named a black female who was believed to deal heavily in heroin. The Narcotics detective car carried four detectives. The atmosphere was tense as they awaited the arrival of a beat car for backup. At a shout from one detective, they all ran to the apartment. The uniformed officer covered the back door as two detectives rushed up the stairs, guns in hand, and the other two searched the lower level for occupants. The woman named on the warrant was not present. Only the babysitter and a small infant were in the dwelling. A thorough search failed to uncover any drugs. The dramatic precautionary measures of five police officers with weapons drawn appeared almost ludicrous in the quiet apartment.

The other type of bust is even more dramatic and tense--the buy and bust. As the case outlined below indicates, the buy and bust can also be a comedy of errors.

Two Atlanta "narcs" had been buying small quantities of drugs from two white males during the previous weeks. They had arranged to meet the dealers at a gas station in Dekalb County. One agent was to purchase several pounds of marijuana; the other was buying a large quantity of cocaine. At 5:30 p.m. one July evening, a total of sixteen Narcotics agents gathered at a predesignated location. Included were Atlanta Narcotics detectives, Dekalb County and Cobb County agents. The two undercover buyers were outfitted with hidden radio equipment. Signals were discussed and it was decided that if an agent opened the car's trunk, all backup should move in. At the last moment confusion reigned; since they expected to separate, which car would follow which agent? Which unit would have the receiver for which agent's transmitter? Finally, these problems were resolved, and the four cars separated.

The dealers arrived at the contact point, but instead of separating, both got into the agents' car which drove off, followed by the three backup cars. Almost immediately, one of the backup units got separated from the rest; and everyone laughed at the inefficiency of Cobb County. A few minutes later the unit directly behind the buyers radioed the other backup car to take over. The latter lost sight of the undercover agents' car by the time it had assumed the tail position. The intercar radio equipment began to malfunction, making communication between backup units impossible. Reception of the hidden transmitters was also impossible since they only carry over a short range. The next hour and a half was spent searching for the buyers' car and the other backup cars. It seemed both hopeless and hilarious.

By some miracle the buyers and dealers were spotted in a driveway several blocks from the original meet. Central radio was called and asked to notify the other counties' agents. Soon the other backup car arrived; the Cobb County car was still missing. The hood went up and the units screeched to a halt in the driveway of the upper-middle-class house. All rushed into the house to find only one of the dealers (age 17), his younger brother, and one Narcotics agent.

Where was the other dealer and Atlanta detective? It was apparent that they had separated from the others. The next hour was spent searching for them. The missing Cobb County unit, which had apparently been in the area, located the sounds of

the missing agent from his hidden microphone and
notified the Atlanta dispatcher who relayed the
message to the other backup units. Using clues such
as the sounds of children and the voice of the agent
requesting a beer, it was decided that a pizza restaurant was the likely spot. Two agents and the
observer entered the restaurant, ordered beers, and
casually surveyed the establishment. They located
the missing agent and dealer.

The next several hours were spent following
them from county to county, house to house, awaiting
the signal for the bust. Finally at 10:00 p.m. the
buying agent indicated through the hidden microphone
that no buy "was coming down." All backup units
dispersed.

Almost five hours had elapsed; sixteen officers
had been employed; one pound of marijuana was purchased; and one teenage dealer arrested. The officers' reaction to the mayhem and misadventure was
that it had been a typical buy and bust.

The Narcotics squad, as indicated in this
brief account, performs more active police work than
the other squads surveyed. Their work also has more
frequent potential risk and excitement although it
is often anticlimactic due to both human and mechan-
ical inefficiency. This squad also largely inter-
acts with a different segment of the population.
Although many cases occur within the lower-class
communities and the housing projects, much time is
also spent outside of city of Atlanta in the middle-
and upper-middle-class suburbs. Thus, the officers
working in the Narcotics squad did not speak as
derogatorily about the lower-class black segment as
the detectives in other squads whose contacts with
that segment were more commonplace.

Other Detective Police Work

Aside from the eight-hour watch that detectives
work five days a week, they often must perform as
police officers at other times. Many officers often

work beyond the eight-hour watch on a case. This is particularly true of Homicide where a detective must exhaust all major leads on a case prior to going off duty. In every squad, calls that come in near the end of the watch must be handled by the same detective through the report writing and the arrest. Until recently, this overtime was not financially compensated. Several years ago, however, the practice of "comp time" was instituted. An officer can build up his hours of overtime and then receive "comp days" which are paid vacation days.

The detective must also appear frequently in court. When an arrest is made, it is possible that the officer will have to appear in three different courts. The initial hearing is at the city munici-pal court, located on the fourth floor of the police station. Except for morning watch personnel, detec-tives are permitted to schedule their appearances for on-duty hours. Thus, Saturday and Sunday are considered as the ideal but difficult to obtain days off since an officer would never have to go to city court on his days off. If the case is bound over, the detective must prepare for, and appear before, the grand jury. If the grand jury indicts the per-petrator, the officer will have to appear in crimi-nal court. These latter court appearances may not occur during on-duty hours, but the police officer must attend. However, he is compensated for court time.

The hours spent in court would not be as frus-trating to officers if they felt that the judicial system was equitable and representative of law and order. However, the typical police view of the court system is expressed in the following statement by a twenty-five year old white male detective:

> The courts are ineffective and uncon-
> trolled. There is far too much discre-
> tion left to the judge and far too much
> red tape. It should be streamlined in
> order to avoid the legal game that law-
> yers and judges play to soak the public.
> There should be a greater effort to

eliminate plea bargaining. There should
be a lot more bench trials that are more
cut and dry. Now, there is undue repetition, and the rules of evidence produce
legal hassles that last half a day. The
pendulum of justice has fallen too far
to the left. They don't care about the
victim anymore.

Thus, with a negative attitude toward the court and
the entire judicial process, the police officer may
have to disrupt his day off to testify. Time after
time, the officers say they see the work and investigation that they have performed prove to be use-
less in the courts. This will be discussed further
in Chapter 7.

Aside from working for the Atlanta Police
Department, many officers also work extra jobs in
order to supplement what they consider a less than
adequate salary. The extra income may help cover
the expenses for diamond rings and fully equipped
vans, two material objects commonly owned by detectives. Although some of the extra jobs are non-
police-related (several officers own small businesses), most involve security-oriented jobs in
which they wear their uniform and gun. Regular
security jobs exist in shopping malls, discount
stores, bars, and clubs. Part-time security employment is available for concerts, sporting events,
and for visits to Atlanta by VIP's. Officers are
also hired by the Atlanta Police Bureau for the off-
duty task of directing traffic during rush hours
and at musical and sporting events.

Between comp time, court time, and extra jobs,
it is not unusual for a police officer to be working seven days a week and up to eighteen hours a
day. Because fatigue among police officers is
endemic, it is not surprising that "cracking" is
commonplace. The effect of long hours upon morale
and physical efficiency must not be overlooked when
examining the attitudes and daily practices of the
detectives.

Females in Detective Work

The males' reception of women in the detective squads appeared to be mixed. The men in all-male squads were verbally grateful that no females were assigned to work with them. The male detectives in the sexually heterogeneous squads tolerated their female peers but were noticeably relieved and more relaxed on the watches when no women were present due to days off. As stated earlier, when a male and female were partners, the former always dominated the partnership: driving the detective car; dictating the activities of the shift; and frequently conducting the interviews of suspects and victims. The female usually did the paper work.

There was no violent encounter during the months of observation. It is therefore difficult to speculate upon male overprotectiveness of female detective partners. However, several males privately stated that they looked upon the women as less than equal partners and regarded their presence in any future violent situation as a hindrance, another force to contend with.

None of the women assigned to the detective division expressed a desire to return to uniform patrol duty. In fact, many stated that they were relieved to be out of uniform and welcomed the relative safety of detective work and their return to "feminine" attire. None seemed to resent the males' dominance, and they always followed the males' lead without verbal complaint. When females rode alone or together without male partners, they did not become more assertive or work oriented. Those observed did a minimal amount of policework: no patrolling or investigative work; only answering radio calls with dispatch. The remainder of their time was spent in personal activities. On calls, the women, either alone or with a male partner, appeared unemotional and aloof from the victims' plight. The females assigned to Sex Crimes were generally unsympathetic to the rape victims. They seemed more skeptical of the latters' veracity than their male partners. This is ironic since most male officers in the sample believe that women should be assigned to Sex Crimes. However, as Chapter 8 will indicate, the female officers have acquired the same type of cynical and negative feelings toward the public as the males have.

The detectives in the Atlanta Police Department are proud of reaching detective rank. There is a distinct hierarchy, and the detective rank, although near the bottom, is a step up. The survey of several squads has shown that a detective's shift does not consist of continuous calls and investigation. There are also few occasions when their work has the drama and excitement which the term detective connotes to the general public. Calls are usually routine and involve merely writing up a report with little or no follow-up work. The segment of the public that most detectives interact with is generally the lower-class black. Daily, the officer, male or female, finds himself in an alien subculture; the norms and social structure of the group often diametrically opposed to the officer's values. The hours, the cases, and the people encountered all contribute to the creation of a unique profession. After examining the policing activities of the uniformed officer, the effects of belonging in this police subculture upon attitudes and behavior will be discussed.

5

UNIFORMED OFFICERS' POLICING ACTIVITIES

The uniformed officers usually arrive at their zone headquarters a quarter to a half hour prior to the actual watch change. This time is spent signing out a radio, picking up blank report forms, and in conversation with peers and sergeants. As stated previously, the groups that form before roll call are usually segregated racially. The few female officers present appear to be accepted at this level of interaction, easily joining in the discussions of grievances and pleasantries.[1] Twice a week all watch officers must arrive twenty minutes early for roll call training. The course of instruction consists of the senior sergeant reading a section from the procedural handbook.

Promptly at three o'clock on evening watch the officers form ranks. The degree of military procedure varies from zone to zone, depending upon the watch lieutenant and his wishes. In one precinct, for example, the officers casually remain seated during roll call; in another, two straight lines are formed and the officers are told to stand at attention. Attendance is taken; the men are inspected by a sergeant or the lieutenant; cars and beats are assigned to the roustabouts; and any information pertinent to the watch is given.

Unlike roll calls in Philadelphia (Rubinstein 1973), Los Angeles (Wambaugh 1970, 1972), and in films, it is extremely rare for stolen autos and descriptions of fugitives to be announced. There

---

[1]The distribution of females on evening watch in the zones I observed were: zone 2--2 white females, 1 black female; zone 5--0 white females, 2 black females; zone 1--2 white females, 1 black female; zone 3--1 white female, 0 black females. In addition there were 2 white female recruits: 1 in zone 5 and 1 in zone 3.

is, in fact, little communication between watches.
Police-related announcements given at roll call in
Atlanta are mostly restricted to transmitting general warnings and information from detective squads.
For example, the sergeant might indicate that the
Intelligence Squad has ascertained that a certain
nightclub is a center for underworld activity and
desires uniformed officers assigned to the area to
keep it under observation. The sergeant also passes
on requests for patrolling activity made to him by
private citizens.

Immediately after dismissal the officers go
outside to await the arrival of the day watch car
for their assigned beat. The day watch cars are
frequently waiting in line outside the zone building.
However, an officer may have to wait for several
minutes since the day watch officer on his beat may
still be out of service on a call. The watch change
is conducted quickly and formally.

After getting into their cars the officers are
faced with eight hours of "work" ahead, a time that
can be boring and tedious or exciting and full of
action. The hours may be spent busily handling
policing duties or pursuing more personal interests.
All police work must be duly recorded on the officer's activity sheet, citing signals received,
locations, and times initiated and completed.

Prior to examining in detail the actual policing duties, the activities that are not actually
assigned work but do comply in some sense with regulations will be surveyed. These practices are
fairly well institutionalized. They are eagerly
anticipated by the officers with much thought given
to how, when, and where to schedule them in the
shift.

Regulations prescribe only one coffee break
per officer's watch although in reality several are
taken. The first stop for coffee and/or a snack is
often taken within the first hour of the watch, unless the officer is tied up on a call. There are
several restaurants in all the zones that dispense
free coffee to police officers, a practice that has

been outlawed by the present administration. Officers attempt to take their breaks at these locations since one or more other officers will usually be present. Technically, one is supposed to remain within the boundaries of one's beat. This rule is circumvented frequently during the watch; the first occasion may be to have coffee at a hashery in an adjoining beat. The break is supposed to consume only ten minutes. It may in fact last well over thirty minutes if no calls are received. Niederhoffer (1969) hypothesizes that this initial coffee break is a ritual that may act to minimize the anxiety the officer faces daily. He states that "the ceremonious interruption, like a religious duty, may constitute a libation to the Gods" (Niederhoffer 1969: 220).

The officers also stop in for coffee while still officially out on a call. Acting against the rules, they may sit in the restaurant either completing the report or, if it is already finished, drinking coffee leisurely and then notifying radio that they are back in service.

The dinner stop, the 27, cannot be taken until three hours of the watch have passed. The officers must ask the dispatcher for permission to eat since a certain number of cars must be in service in each sector. Permission is usually granted and the officer indicates to radio the location of his stop. Although out of service, his radio is kept on since a distress call can take place at any time.[2] On the infrequent busy nights when the calls come in one after another, an officer may not be able to take his dinner break until near the end of the watch. Much thought and deliberation is always given to where to eat. The half-price restaurants (again, against rules) are given top priority.

---

[2]One signal 63 (officer in trouble) occurred while an officer and I were eating dinner, the former overtly relaxed and not listening to his radio. He was instantly aware of the 63 and moved so swiftly that we were the second car on the scene.

An officer rarely dines alone. By prior arrangement, either at the precinct or at a meeting during the watch, several officers agree to meet for dinner. The rules dictate that only two cars can pull out at the same location. However, there are frequently more than two police vehicles outside one establishment although only two have officially pulled out at that location. The few sergeants who maintain relationships of camaraderie with their men often eat dinner with them. The food break is supposed to last a maximum of thirty minutes. Officers often circumvent this rule by pulling back into service after a half hour and remaining in the restaurant for a prolonged period of time--perhaps until they receive a radio call.

At some point during the watch, each officer requests permission to go to the city shop to get gasoline. This also appears to be an eagerly anticipated break in the routine. It allows the officers to leave not only the confines of their beats but also to leave the zone. It is also one of the rare times in the daily schedule when one has the opportunity to encounter officers from other zones. The pull-out time to the shop may be extended by adding in the radio request that one's car is in need of repairs which may or may not be true. The trip to the city shop is occasionally used as a rendezvous point between male and female officers who work in different zones.

The 59 (meet an officer) has been alluded to earlier. The importance for morale of these meetings between officers cannot be minimized. Several of the new sergeants have attempted to limit the number of 59's, an action that has met with overt hostility and noncompliance. The 59 may be requested on radio. An officer calls another beat officer and names an intersection asking if the latter is free for a 59. Or, it may take place spontaneously as two cars pass on the street and automatically pull over.

There is a standard tactical placement to the 59. Cars are always side by side facing in opposite directions. This position allows the officers to watch all directions, and it also places the drivers next to each other. Frequently these meetings grow in size as either another car passes by and joins the group, or other officers hear the 59 request and intentionally travel to the site. If the officers intend to have a lengthy bull session they will arrange to meet behind certain buildings or in other places that are secluded from the eyes of the public and the brass. Occasionally refreshments such as donuts and coffee are brought to these large gatherings. An officer from another zone occasionally appears at these 59's, thus providing conversational items such as comparing the sergeants and the policies of the different zones. It is rare for a black officer to be present at a white 59. Female officers are overtly accepted, although one hears at least one male in the group complain to another about her presence.

The main theme of discussion at these meetings concerns the politics of the police department. Dissatisfaction with the commissioner and with the zone's brass are aired ad nauseam. Other topics include joking about recent calls, stories about past exploits, and sexual joking and discussion. On an average night one officer may be involved in up to ten 59's with only a few announced on radio. The 59's exemplify the solidarity among the white uniformed officers and reinforce their ties of camaraderie daily.

The last regulation non-policing activities to be discussed include those activities that have some policing rationale overtly, but are not usually performed for that ostensible purpose. Most officers whose beats include topless lounges or other types of bars frequently leave their cars and spend some time in these establishments. Their overt aim is to patrol and prevent any illegal activities from taking place. However, the length of time spent observing the dancers and waitresses seems to indicate a more personal and prurient motivation.

Several officers bring CB radios to work with them and place them in the squad cars. The officers enjoy parking on the median or at the side of

one of Atlanta's main thoroughfares and listening
to the truck drivers describe the "local yokel" or
the "pokey smokey" (a reference to the poor job performance of the city cars). The officers' vehicles
are not equipped with radar and they seldom chase
errant motorists. Their expressed purpose in spending hours sitting in their vehicles by a highway is
to slow traffic down by their presence. But they
also enjoy the conversation and repartee with the
CBers.

Lastly, a disproportionate amount of time is
spent by both uniformed officers and detectives
cruising the city parks looking for homosexual
solicitors. Flashlights are used to illuminate
couples in cars, searching for two homosexuals.
Apparently the ideal object of the search is to
locate two men in the process of solicitation or
sexual activity. The outcome involves much police
"man"handling--referred to by police officers as
"jacking up queers." The police rationale is to
rid the city streets of homosexual perversion. The
more covert explanation is not within the scope of
this anthropological study but undoubtedly psychological studies could reveal the explanation for the
almost fanatical hatred of homosexuals expressed by
male officers.

Policing Duties

The officers do spend some time patrolling the
area of their beats. This activity should, according to the rules, take up all of the officer's
watch, only to be interrupted by calls or for dinner. In reality, cruising up and down city streets
is tedious and unexciting. Given the present low
level of motivation, the white uniformed officers
do not generally fulfill this function to the
degree required by the regulations. Black male
officers may be performing more in the ideal manner.
One black male observed for several evenings checked
almost every building on his beat nightly. He
drove behind all the warehouses checking doors and
noting license tags. He expressed the view that
the beat was his responsibility and that the

94

people who resided there were depending upon him. It is extremely rare for a white officer to patrol in this fashion or to express a similar sense of obligation to the citizenry.

While driving around, it is not uncommon for an officer to be waved down by someone in need of a police officer's assistance. Infrequently, a report is taken, in which case the officer notifies radio that he is out of service. For example, one evening a white male officer was hailed by a white middle-aged female who hysterically complained that her two teenage sons were fighting. The officer went to her apartment and listened for several minutes. The source of friction appeared to be the death of the father a few days earlier. When the officer attempted to mediate and was continuously inter-rupted, he still maintained a calm and interested manner. Finally he advised the boys to go out separately and cool off. No report was taken and the officer pulled in to radio, code 12 (investi-gated).

While patrolling, police officers are supposed to be on the alert for traffic and parking viola-tions. Most white officers, expressing an attitude of "Why should I do any work?", seldom write cita-tions except in accident cases. From time to time the watch sergeants, at roll call, encourage the officers to put more energy into traffic cases. At one zone the officers were aware that a certain number of tickets were expected to be handed in weekly. Dispensing traffic violations involves another court appearance for the uniformed officer. Since (s)he decides the court date and time, the officer is usually able to schedule all traffic cases on two mornings a month.

Discretion is a definite aspect of traffic work. Several white officers, observing a flagrant violation by a white motorist, did not pull him over, thereby openly expressing their racial selec-tion of violators. Having pulled over a car, offi-cers commonly issued citations to black drivers while white motorists received only verbal warnings.

95

The uniformed officer spends much of the watch backing up other officers on calls. Occasionally another officer is designated by radio to back up, but more frequently the officer goes independently. (S)he may or may not notify the dispatcher of his intentions. There are several reasons why a police officer may hurry to arrive at another's call. Boredom is a major factor. Attendance at the scene offers both the opportunity to converse with another officer and the potential for some excitement. The backup may also be the result of the type of call. On any call involving death, even a "natural," many officers appear. Although there may be no threat of danger associated with the signal, deaths attract police officers. On any signal that may involve violent activity, the officers want to accompany their friends, even though the rulebook may not dictate the necessity. of supportive units. For example, on most signal 29's (fight) support is given. The location of the call is another factor. In a housing project after dark, all officers are aware of the element of danger and will hasten to their colleague's assistance although neither (s)he nor radio has requested it.

Whom one backs up is self-selective to a certain extent, limited only by the geographic position of the beats. Females are generally provided with more backup. (This will be dealt with extensively in Chapter 8.) Voluntary backups are rarely interracial. The white officer often wants to make an appearance at another white officer's call in order to further solidify the camaraderie that exists between them. However, the sociopolitical climate involves such a degree of racial polarization that not only will a white officer not freely back up a black officer but several have indeed expressed the view that they would not hurry to arrive at an officer-in-trouble signal that involved a black officer.

The main policing duty that cannot be avoided by any officer is handling the calls dispatched specifically to him or her. The number of calls an officer receives per watch varies from beat to beat; by the day of the week; and, according to police folklore, by the time of the month. A patrolman may handle only one call on a watch; another night (s)he may be continuously swamped and receive up to fifteen different cases. Friday and Saturday nights are the most active; hence only officers with either much seniority or political clout receive them as off-days. Police officers believe that crime rates increase after the welfare checks are received at the beginning of the month, providing the recipients with funds for alcohol. It is also a firm aspect of police mythology that violent acts increase during the full moon.

The type of calls generally received also varies from area to area. As one might expect, the beat officers in the few elite areas of the city handle mostly burglary and information calls. This will be elaborated upon further below.

Whenever an officer is assigned to a call, (s)he must ultimately terminate his activity on it with a code number to the dispatcher. The code, representing how the call was handled, is usually an automatic response to the specific signal involved. For example code 17 means that a report has been taken. On every burglary or robbery case it is understood by the officers that the calls will be handled with code 17. Perhaps the most popular pull-in code is 12, which means the situation has been investigated but that no paper work had to be done. Since people often call in false reports to the department, a code 22 (unable to locate address or caller) or a code 13 (no such number) is not uncommon. There are twenty-seven possible codes, although the ones above are the most frequently used.

There are eighty-six different signals that a uniformed officer may have to respond to. A summary of the most frequent signals follows, citing actual examples from fieldwork experiences.

Signal 39 (Information for Officer)

This is considered to be the most potentially

dangerous signal to respond to since it is the catch-all signal and conveys little information to the officer. The most recent death of an on-duty officer at the time of the study had occurred on a signal 39. Examples will be given below since they serve to exemplify the broad range of citizens' expectations and the spectrum of activities that are involved in uniformed policing.

January 15 (one white male; affluent beat)-- Signal 39 involved a man's complaint concerning the barking of a neighbor's dog which was preventing him from sleeping. The police officer went back and forth between the neighbors attempting to nego- tiate a peace settlement. The call consumed almost 45 minutes and was regarded as a nuisance by the officer.

January 21 (one white male; lower-middle- class beat)--A white male had called for a police officer because he was upset that his wife had left him. He wanted the officer to talk to her but did not know where she was. Several hours later, received another signal 39 at the same address. The husband had located his wife. The officer went to speak to her and reported back to the caller that she emphatically refused to return home. No report was taken and the officer noted that many lower class people regard police personnel as mar- riage and family counselors. This is a complaint made quite frequently by the uniformed officers.

January 27 (one white male; lower-middle- class beat)--Officer spoke to a white female who was concerned about a car that had been parked in front of her home for a week. Officer checked with radio to see if vehicle was on the stolen list; it was not. He then called for a tow truck and filled out two reports; an auto impound and a miscellaneous incident report.

February 3 (one white male; downtown beat)-- A young white couple, tourists, were unable to locate their car which they had parked on a down- town street. The officer drove them up and down the streets of downtown Atlanta for over an hour until the vehicle was found.

February 24 (one white male; downtown beat)--
White male caller stated that a man was unconscious
in the bushes. Police officer investigated and
found the "victim" to be a wino who had passed out.
Officer roused the man and threw him into the back
seat of the squad car. Since the jail is located
in the downtown zone, officers often transport
prisoners instead of calling for a wagon. First an
arrest report and a copy of the charges has to be
filled out. In this case it was difficult because
the prisoner was unable to recall his name or
address. "John Doe" of the "Mission" was driven to
the city jail where he was deposited with some
difficulty by the officer and a city employee.

February 27 (one white male; downtown beat)--
Black female desired a police escort from a downtown building because she believed that her estranged husband was waiting for her in the lobby.
The officer walked out of the building with her but
later commented upon the services that "these people
expect from the police."

March 2 (one white male; downtown beat)--
Called to the Hilton Hotel by an irate white male
who had been stuck in a Hilton elevator and wanted
to know if he could have someone arrested or sue
the hotel. The officer patiently explained that
there were no grounds for arrest and that if the
man required legal advice he should see an attorney.
No report was taken.

March 13 (one white female; lower-middle-
class beat)--Caller was a civilian employee of the
police department who was unhappy about the neighborhood children throwing objects into her yard.
The officer spent several minutes socially chatting
but did not visit the parents of the children. She
later commented that the woman was a bit of a 24
(demented person).

March 18 (one white male; lower-middle-
class beat)--Call concerned mischievious behavior
by children in a trailer park. The caller

identified three children by name and indicated
their trailers to the officer. The latter then
went to all three mobile homes and spoke to the
mothers and/or fathers advising them of the situation. No report taken.

March 24 (one white male; affluent beat)--The
officer handled a frequently received complaint in
upper-class areas concerning teenagers' mischief
with the garbage cans, known as "herbie-curbies"
since they are put out near the curb for pick-up.
A common practice among adolescents in these areas
involves hitting the garbage cans with their cars.
The officer solicitously told the white female complainant that he was keeping an eye out for the
herbie-curbie offenders.

March 31 (one white male; upper-middle-class
beat)--Call was to a mental hospital to speak to a
distraught middle-aged white female. She was the
mother of a fifteen-year-old girl whom she had
brought for admittance to the private clinic. The
girl had run away from home repeatedly in order to
live with her boyfriend and was purportedly heavily
involved with drugs. The officer spent the next
hour driving around the neighborhood, going into
restaurants and stores in search of the girl. He
also put a signal 78 (description) on the radio.
The subject was not located and a miscellaneous
report was taken.

Signal 41 (Investigate Automobile Accident)

It is extremely rare for a police officer to
work two days in a row without receiving a "wreck"
call. Almost every officer dislikes the 41 and
therefore warily regards rainy days and nights when
more accidents occur. The source of the officers'
antipathy lies in the amount of paper work involved
with a signal 41. An accident report must always
be filled out unless the incident took place on
private property. This report must contain the
vehicles' identification numbers, tag numbers, inspection numbers, and odometer reading for all
vehicles involved. Drivers' license information

for all drivers must be replicated on the report; a
narrative and a drawing of the accident must also
be included. It is a time-consuming report that may
take an hour to complete. According to Georgia law,
in every wreck, a driver must be charged and a court
date set. Therefore, a minimum of one citation must
be written, plus a summons for the other driver(s).
If the accident also involves a person driving under
the influence of alcohol (signal 30) many citations
may be given. An arrest report must be filled out;
a copy of charges; an auto impound report; a property management report if there are any articles
in the car that must be turned in; plus the prisoner
must be transported first to Grady Hospital for
alcohol content testing and then to the city jail.
An accident involving a DUI may keep an officer out
of service for several hours and often results in
overtime.

Most officers seem to resent the monotony and
predictability of the 41 although several females
express a more positive attitude toward wreck calls.
The 41 seems to be one particular type of signal
that these females feel they are handling as efficiently as the males.

Signal 45 (Investigate Larceny)

Signal 45's are common and tend to be a routine
matter of writing up a crime against property
report. CB radios in Atlanta during 1976 were
the most common objects of theft. Police officers
were frequently called to parking lots by vehicle
owners who had discovered a broken window or other
sign of forcible entry and the loss of their CB
radios. The CB racket was so rampant and known to
the police that one evening an officer actually pre-
dicted a theft. Patrolling a certain parking lot
he noted that he would not be surprised if one of
the many cars sporting a CB antenna was the object
of a theft that evening. Several hours later, he
received a call to that lot to take a report from
an irate citizen who had discovered that his CB
equipment had been taken. In recording the data
required on these larceny reports both the officer

and the victim are well aware that recovery of the
stolen property is unlikely. In most cases the
report is taken for insurance purposes.

Other than CB's, 45 calls may involve clothing
removed from vehicles, spare tires, auto batteries
and hubcaps, and wallets. Shoplifting is a common
offense that is dispatched to the officer as a
signal 45. Most major department stores employ
their own security force, including many off-duty
city police who fill out the necessary reports.
Therefore, the only duty of the on-duty officer is
transportation of the offenders, if juveniles, to
the juvenile detention center. During the months
of observation, most 45 victims were white and
appeared to be fairly affluent. The officers always
appeared sympathetic and duly recorded the pertinent
data. After the victim's departure, the officers
frequently commented upon either the stupidity of
the victim or the ostentatiousness that had provoked the theft.

Signals 3 and 65 (Alarm Ringing)

During the seven months observing the Uniform
division, alarm signals were a common phenomena.
Invariably false alarms, they are set off inadver-
tently by departing employees at the end of the
day; wind; electrical storms; and by faulty wiring.
The signals usually originate from a commercial
enterprise, although occasionally the alarm is
located in an affluent private dwelling. The uniformed officer has a certain procedure to follow.
He must check all windows and doors for signs of
entry. The manner in which this was performed
varied from the rare individual who left the car to
manually investigate all apertures and on occasion
even climbed onto roofs to check for entry to the
officer who, from the squad car, cursorily shone
his flashlight on the building. Having ascertained
that no forcible entry has been made, the officer
notifies radio and is usually directed to remain at
the site until the alarm is reset either by the
owner or the alarm company. This may keep the officer out of service for an additional half hour

until (s)he pulls in code 12, investigated.

Signal 28 (Drunk)

The drunk call in Atlanta is a basic part of the uniformed officer's watch. The perpetrator in most of the cases is not the middle-class citizen who has had too much to drink, but it is the wino, an individual for whom alcohol has become a way of life and for whom arrests and short stays in city jails are common. As with the lower-class black subculture, the police officer dealing with the 28's is encountering an alien life-style. The officer, seeing, smelling, and listening to the filth and incoherence of the drunk, appears to react either with humor or aggression. The manner of reaction seems to vary with the type of drunk. The happy and relatively polite 28 is joked with;[3] the ones who have passed out or are obnoxious are often treated roughly.

The joking that takes place with winos may at first appear cruel and inhuman to the non-police observers. "Inhuman" is an appropriate label since it appears that extensive contact with winos makes it impossible for the police to regard the drunk as human. The rookie may see the pitiable condition of a human being, but continued exposure to the wino life-style eradicates any feelings of pity and (s)he begins to view the drunk as somewhat less than human, a ready victim for pent up hostilities and frustrations.

January 8 (one white male; lower-middle-class beat)--Called to the front of a run-down hotel where a very intoxicated white male was lying on the ground. The officer dragged him into the car which was soon heavy with the odors of uncleanliness,

---

[3]I was frequently made a part of these jokes with officers pretending that I had just been raped by the prisoner.

alcohol, and vomit. After filling out the arrest report with some difficulty, since the white male had trouble communicating, the officer transported him to the city jail. During the ride the officer asked the prisoner the usual police/drunk questions:

> Are you guilty of fornicating with an aardvark? (The usual response varies from, "No sir, not me," to "I don't know no aardvarks.")
>
> Are you in possession of a rape tool?
>
> Are you in possession of a dead tool?

Occasionally the prisoner may be more alert and respond aggressively, accusing the officer of harassment. More often, however, the drunk is either oblivious to the game or begins to cry and deny any guilt.

January 16 (one white female; lower-middle-class beat)--The drunk was a young white male, age twenty-four, who had been behaving offensively to passersby. Instead of manhandling him and forcibly getting him into the car, the female utilized a verbal strategy asking the 28 if he wanted to go for a ride to a local hamburger restaurant. Without resistance he entered the squad car. This officer also enjoyed joking with the drunk, teasing him about what they would do later in the evening and about where he preferred to be dropped off.

January 23 (one white female; middle-class beat)--The signal 28 was not a usual call since the drunk was in the same building as a "cop killer" who had recently been discharged from the state mental hospital. All officers had been warned at roll call several days before about the address. A male motorman appeared at the same time as the squad car. He led the way into the building and assisted in bringing the white male drunk down the stairs and into the car. Later the female officer admitted that she had been relieved to see a male officer arrive at the scene.

February 6 (one white male; downtown beat)--
The downtown beats handle the most signal 28's even
though the downtown foot patrol also spend most of
their watch arresting public drunks. The officer
saw a man lying in the detective lot of the police
station. Having ascertained that the male was
intoxicated, he pulled out of service on a signal
28. After completing the arrest reports, the officer laughed about the considerateness of the
prisoner--passing out in front of the station.
Shortly after depositing that 28 at the jail the
officer received another signal 28 to an office
building where a security guard informed him that
an old black male was lying in the men's room. The
arrestee was escorted to the car with some difficulty, the report written, and the 28 transported
to the jail. The officer commented that two drunks
in a row were too much; he went to wash his hands
and remarked upon how filthy 28's made him feel.

June 11 (one white male; lower-class beat)--
An atypical 28 call since it involved a white male
whose clothing and speech indicated a middle-class
life-style and nonwino behavior pattern. However,
the officer checked his record through radio and
discovered a lengthy number of drunk arrests. The
prisoner's attitude was also unusual. Aggressively
he demanded to be driven home immediately throughout the ride to the jail, varying from a condescending to a supplicating manner.

Signal 29 (Disorder or Fight)

Signal 29's include a broad variety of situations as the incidents depicted below will illustrate. In domestic 29's, involving people known to
each other, no report or arrest is usually made,
and the officer attempts to act as mediator or just
as a sounding board. (S)he may advise one member of
the dispute to take out a warrant, in which case (s)he
would pull in code 5 (domestic situation, advised a
warrant). Although the domestic 29 does not often
involve danger for the law enforcement officer,
another unit often backs up since most signal 29's
originate in the black housing projects where lower-

class blacks apparently perceive the police officer as a family counselor or mediator. The most frequent disputes in these cases are between husband and wife, and between mother and daughter. Alcohol is a common aspect of the signal 29, hence many calls are dispatched as signals 29, 28.

January 17 (one white female; lower-class beat)--Received signal 29 to a project. A male officer immediately announced on radio that he would also go to the call. The female was the first on the scene and after being confronted with an apartment crowded with adults and children, she merely asked if everything was O.K. now. Someone said yes, and the officer left after telling two boys to stop fighting on the steps. The officer drove away from the project after talking to the male backup who had not appeared in time to accompany her to the apartment. Several minutes later, shortly before the watch change, the officer received another signal 29 at the same address. This time the male officer arrived first and dominated the situation. A fight had broken out in the yard and the male officer arrested two individuals. He told the female officer to transport one prisoner to the jail. She complied and expressed appreciation for the backup although she later confided a resentment for his usurpation of her call.

January 18 (one white male; lower-class beat)-- Call involved an intoxicated middle-aged white female whose head was bleeding profusely. Six police officers arrived at the scene since the information conveyed by radio had included the fact that an injury had occurred. She claimed that her male roommate had hit her on the head. Since the victim was obnoxious and belligerent, refusing to go to the hospital for treatment, the officers left quickly. They stood outside the building for several minutes joking about the victim's delusions (she claimed that her father was the president of a major oil company) and the filthy condition of her home. No report was taken.

January 30 (one white male; lower-middle-class beat)--The caller was an irate white male whose wife

had locked him out of the house. The officer first
spoke to him and attempted to calm him down; then
the officer went into the house to speak to the
woman. He emerged with a suitcase and instructed
the male to leave the area immediately. The interactions had taken almost an hour with the officer
functioning as a sounding board for domestic grievances.

February 12 (one white male; downtown beat)--
Called to a housing project where the officer was
confronted by three black females, one of whom requested that the officer eject her "friend" from
the apartment. After listening to each woman yell
and interrupt the other, the officer warned them to
settle down saying that if he received another call,
an arrest would be made. He then left, privately
remarking that the call had been a typical 29. This
officer's threat to arrest someone if there was further trouble is a frequent exit line made by officers at 29's.

February 13 (one white male; downtown beat)--
Received a signal 29 to the YMCA. Another car
backed up since the information included a signal
24 (demented person). The officers located the
manager who was attempting to evict an aged white
male who was manifesting bizarre behavior--walking
in the lobby in his underwear, talking to himself.
The officers assisted him in packing his few be-
longings and escorted him to the eighth floor of
Grady Hospital, the psych ward.

March 11 (one white male; lower-middle-class
beat)--Officer received a signal 29/69, fight with
person(s) armed. Another car immediately notified
radio that it would back up. At the scene, the
officers found a white, middle-aged married couple
engaged in an argument outside their house; the
husband holding a hoe which the wife claimed he had
threatened her with. The woman had called the
police. As usual on a domestic 29, the officer
insisted that each disputant tell his/her story
without interruption. (This is actually a difficult task--the police officer constantly has to tell
the people to "shut up.") After hearing both sides

of the argument, the officer told the couple to calm down and suggested that the woman go visit a neighbor or nearby relative for a short time. He also warned them that if he received another call, they would both be arrested.

May 21 (one white male; lower-class beat)-- Signal 29 originated in a housing project. Disputants were two black females, mother and daughter. The former had called the department, claiming that her daughter was throwing glassware at her. The officer ascertained that the dispute centered on the younger woman's welfare check which the mother had apparently hidden in order that it would not be spent on alcohol. The officer advised the older woman to hand over the check and encouraged both to calm down. Their voices could still be heard as the squad car departed. The officer remarked that the housing project residents call the police in matters that would best be kept and resolved within the family group. Many uniformed officers express amusement and contempt at the content of the arguments and the living conditions.

Signal 67 (Person Down)

This signal is usually accompanied by a code 4 (ambulance on the way). Invariably during the seven months of observation, the "person down" proved to be an unconscious drunk. The officer would cancel the ambulance, call for the wagon and write an arrest report for public drunk.

One 67 call deviated from this pattern. The victim was a white male who had suffered an epileptic attack at his home. The officer's only function was to await the arrival of the ambulance. This call was significant since the living conditions encountered closely emulated the most ill-kept apartments in black projects. However, the officer did not make the usual derogatory comments about the filth or the number of seemingly neglected children. When questioned about his feelings concerning their way of life, his only remark was that they were just "poor white rednecks."

Signal 48 (Investigate Dead Person)

When anyone in Atlanta dies outside a hospital, the police department must be called. As stated earlier, several cars invariably arrive, even at the scene of a natural death.

January 17 (one white female; lower-class beat)--Signal 48 received from a government housing project. A backup unit accompanied the female officer but departed after several minutes since the death was apparently a natural; a black male who had recently been discharged from the hospital with cancer. The officer had to remain in the apartment for almost an hour since she had difficulty contacting the medical examiner. During the wait, she collected the hospital card and medication of the deceased in order to write the miscellaneous report. She later expressed pity for the many children and infants who had been awake at almost midnight.

The preceding has been a brief summary of the most frequent types of signals handled by the uniformed officer. In order to further depict their policing duties, ten watches will be surveyed. A sample is being presented in lieu of a complete six-month log because there is little variation in the type of call received. For the entire six months, the average number of calls handled per officer observed was six. This does not include all calls received by the officers since some are cancelled en route.

The main differences in the situations encountered appear to be a result of the socioeconomic level of the officer's beat. The few officers who patrol in affluent areas handle fewer calls, and the events confronted tend to involve less violence, with the callers conforming more closely to the police officers' mores and life-style. The first three evenings presented below illustrate the officers' role and duties in the more elite areas of Atlanta. The remaining shifts described took place in lower-middle- and lower-class beats.

January 15 (one white male)--Four signals
were handled during the watch. First a signal 3,
a silent alarm in a private home, was received.
No one was located on the premises. The officer
checked all doors and windows and pulled in code 12
(investigated). The next call, a 39 concerning dogs
barking has been described above. The next incident
involved a burning car; the officer had only to
await the arrival of the fire department. Lastly,
the beat car was summoned to another private home
which had been the scene of a burglary. This call
was received just before 9:30, to the officer's
chagrin; he had intended to watch a particular television program at a fire station. Entry had been
made with a brick through a window but no property
had been taken. A crime against property report
was taken. Total time out of service (on calls) was
approximately one and a half hours.

March 24 (one white male)--The first call was
on a signal 39 to an affluent private home. The
owner wished to complain about the "herbie curbie"
offenders. Next, the officer handled a typical
accident report (no injuries, one driver obviously
in the wrong). A signal 67 (person down) at a
private home typically involved an intoxicated person. However, in this instance it was a wealthy
woman outside her own home; no arrest or report was
made. Near the end of the shift, the officer received a burglary in progress signal which proved
to be the imagination of an elderly woman who had
heard noises outside her home. No report was taken,
but the officer spent several minutes walking
around the grounds and assuring the caller that she
was safe. Total time out of service was approximately one and three-quarter hours.

March 31 (one white male)--First call involved the runaway teenager from the mental hospital
discussed earlier. The second signal was a 39: a
doctor wanted the officer to sign a certificate
necessary to obtain an auto registration for a used
vehicle. The last call was a larceny report taken
from a secretary whose wallet had been removed from
her purse sometime during her hours working. Total
time out of service was approximately two hours.

February 3 (one white male)--Received eight
calls in this downtown beat. The first, an auto
accident, was nonexistent by the time the officer
arrived. (This occurs frequently since after someone notifies the police of a wreck, the drivers may
mutually decide to leave the scene. The officer
returns to service code 4 (cancel call).) Next, a
report was taken from an elderly white male residing in a run-down hotel. He claimed that his wallet
had been taken by a young black male who frequented
the hotel lobby. The third call has been described
elsewhere as the case of the "lost car" in which
much time was spent searching for a young couple's
vehicle. Then, the officer handled a typical auto
accident report. Having completed it, to his dis-
may, he received another wreck call. However, upon
arrival at the scene he found an officer from an
adjacent zone taking the report. The officer was
next dispatched to a small business where the burglar alarm had gone off. He investigated, but
found no sign of entry. Then an information for
officer signal sent the beat car to the headquarters
office of a major railroad where a black male had
been found trespassing by the private security force.
The latter recognized the perpetrator as a fugitive
suspect on several rape cases. The beat officer
called for a Sex Crimes unit and turned the perpetrator over to the detectives. It might be noted
that it took some time for the detectives to arrive,
and the uniformed officer commented that it was
typical. Total time out of service was approximately four hours.

February 4 (one white male)--Started out the
watch with radio dispatching the car to Grady
Hospital where the officer was directed to write
parking tickets (winnipegs) on vehicles illegally
parked in front of the hospital. Two accidents were
handled by the officer during his shift. Two alarm
calls were received; both proved to be false. A
typical 29, a fight between a husband and wife in a
project, was mediated. The watch ended at the railroad office where the officer made two arrests for
criminal trespass and for possible possession of
marijuana. He took the alleged drug to the property
office and turned it in for analysis. Total time

out of service was approximately three hours.

February 12 (one white male)--Very busy watch
with thirteen calls dispatched to the officer.
These included two false alarms; two drunk signals;
two larcenies, both involving CB radios; and one
fight call between black females in a project.
There were several less typical calls. The first
was a hit-and-run in which a six-year-old boy was
killed by a truck. The officer became depressed and
expressed contempt for the crowd of curiosity seek-
ers who gathered around the body, gasping when
police or medical personnel removed the covering
sheet. The officer spent more than an hour at this
location, measuring skid marks and other distances
required for the report. Later in the evening a
notorious homicide fugitive was reportedly seen at
a grocery store, and the car was among several dispatched to the location. The officers were tense,
but a thorough search failed to reveal the fugitive.
Immediately following this episode, another beat car
became involved in the chase of a drunk driver. The
officer notified radio that he was joining the chase
and spent the next ten minutes with blue light flashing, siren wailing, traveling through downtown
Atlanta at high speeds--and visibly enjoying every
moment of it. The DUI was arrested, but the paper
work was performed by the first beat car who had
initiated the chase. Total time out of service was
approximately three and a half hours.

February 25 (one white male)--Other than one
accident, one alarm call, two larcenies that involved transportation of juvenile offenders, and a
panhandling call, several less common incidents were
handled. A shooting victim, a black male, was interviewed at Grady Hospital. The victim refused to
give any information about the perpetrator. A stabbing call, occurring between two winos outside the
Mission, resulted in further violence. The perpetrator, extremely inebriated, was obnoxious and surely
to the officers. One officer pushed him and the perpetrator hit his head on the sidewalk. He was unconscious with a heavy flow of blood. It was tacitly
understood by all police personnel present that the
wino had slipped. A signal 29, involving several

households of white lower-class adults resulted in
the mass arrest of eight people by the seven police
officers present. As stated earlier, arrests at a
fight call are unusual. In this case, one officer
turned to the others and said, "Let's just arrest
everybody. I'm sick of listening to this _____."
The oldest arrestee, an eighty-year-old female,
resisted and was carried, screaming obscenities, to
a squad car by two officers. Total time out of service was approximately four hours.

March 3 (two black females)--Handled one false
alarm; three drunks, all arrested; a larceny; and
the recovery of stolen property. Also sped to a
help call put in by a foot patrolman who had been
bitten in the leg by a drunk. On the last call of
the shift, the officers transported an aged and
rather senile man, found wandering and crying in the
downtown area, to a contact point with another zone
beat car that would transport him to his nursing
home. Total time out of service was approximately
two and a half hours.

May 17 (one white female)--Handled two accidents; one required the officer to direct traffic
because a traffic light was not functioning. A male
officer passed by, pulled over and instructed the
female to do something else. He proceeded to usurp
her assigned function, claiming that her performance
was inept. Received three information calls, one
resulting in the recovery of a stolen car. Had one
drunk call--an intoxicated black male had been
unable to pay his cab driver. The officer directed
him to the squad car and arrested him for public
drunk. Total time out of service was almost three
hours.

These ten nights presented provide insights
into the number and variety of situations which the
uniformed officer is confronted each day. Few
officers want to be assigned to affluent areas,
although those beats do provide more time for personal pursuits and offer contact with individuals
to whom the officer is better able to relate. However, the lower-middle- and lower-class beats offer

more potential excitement and more situations for an officer to exercise authority and force.

The end of the watch is conducted as militarily as roll call. Unless out of service on a call, the officers spend the last minutes of the shift completing their activity report--adding up the number of calls, time out of service, and hours on duty. When the lieutenant or sergeant calls the watch in, all cars proceed rapidly to the zone headquarters and form a line awaiting their morning watch replacements. They must then go into the building to hand in their walkie-talkies and to give the sergeants their reports. The latter are proofread and must be approved prior to the officers' departure. Errors are not uncommon, particularly with the lengthy accident reports. Thus it is not unusual to see several officers rewriting or correcting their paper work after the watch has changed. After going off duty, some officers frequently meet for outdoor drinking (choir practice)[4], indoor drinking, or for bowling. Others may proceed to a second job at a bar or nightclub.

This chapter has provided a picture of the policing activities performed by uniformed officers. It is important to understand the officers' daily environment. Calls to Uniform patrol mostly involve members of the derelict tramp subculture, the lower-class white (redneck) group, or the blacks residing in government housing. Most officers are not academically trained to regard other groups without ethnocentrism. Even those males and females who have backgrounds that have provided an intellectual understanding of these groups inevitably seem to develop strong prejudices. The inevitability may be the result of both the subcultural values of the

---

[4]The term "choir practice" was a recent addition to Atlanta jargon. It was picked up from Joseph Wambaugh's book which was immensely popular with uniformed officers who passed it around from friend to friend.

police group which emphasize certain groups as the focus of hostility and humor in conversation and behavior, and the repetition of the so-called negative stimuli.

Occasionally, a particularly unusual and humorous incident occurs. This appears to be an essential aspect of policing because humor breaks up the monotony and provides anecdotal material. The following are three examples of calls that acted as emotional stimulants for the officers involved.

The first appeared to be a normal, if somewhat unusually exciting signal, a burglary in progress. Three cars rushed to the home in a well-to-do neighborhood. The distressed female owner who had called the police from a neighbor's house told the officers that upon entering her home she immediately saw signs of wreckage and heard sounds. The officers covered both entrances and flung open the doors to find the perpetrator--a bird that had apparently entered through a window. The subsequent ten minutes were spent waving brooms at the felon in an attempt (successful) to get it through the door.

The following incident may give a further indication of why police officers hold extremely negative attitudes toward drunks. One evening, an officer was called to a bus stop in downtown Atlanta to arrest a white male who was presumably intoxicated and offending passersby. The officer told the man to stand outside the car while he gathered the necessary reports from his briefcase. A few moments later the prisoner unzipped his pants and relieved himself. Many drunks do uncontrollably urinate in the back seat of the police car; however, this incident was unusual since it was an overt, flagrant act. The officer became quite upset and lectured the man about his lack of regard for the sensibilities of the female present. However, he later joked about it during 59's with other officers.

Another amusing, although sad, case might be entitled the "Swiss Cheese Caper." The signal was a burglary at a ramshackle apartment in one of the many impoverished areas of Atlanta. The caller was

an elderly white male whose home was literally
filled from the floor to the ceiling with almost
everything conceivable to the mind, including garbage, clothing, and a vast assortment of unwashed
tableware. The "pseudopartner" began to ask the
usual questions on a crime against property report.
When asked what property had been taken, the victim
seriously stated that Swiss cheese had been stolen
from his refrigerator. He added that the perpetrator had taken only the cheese but had left the
covering paper behind. The report was made; later,
following a hysterical discussion of the call, the
officer ripped up the report. He finally confessed
that the caller was a notorious 24 who faithfully
called the department at least monthly to report
some crime.

Aside from the routine calls and the infrequent
exciting, adrenalin-producing occurrences, therefore, there are occasionally humorous incidents
which seem to help the officers create a psychological defense that enables them to tolerate the
violent acts and the often pitiable condition of the
people that they must encounter daily.

Uniformed Females

Contrary to earlier findings (Sichel, Friedman,
Quint, Smith 1977) the female patrol officers observed did exhibit a different style of patrolling.
In the New York study, the women were described as
neither more nor less likely to use force, draw
weapons or rely on direct orders. In Atlanta, the
female officers observed used force less often than
the males and often avoided giving direct orders.
The New York female officers were more active and
aggressive when partnered with another woman or when
assigned to a precinct in which supervisors were
more receptive to their presence. In the four
Atlanta zones observed, none of the superior officers appeared to appreciate women assigned to
Uniform patrol. Most were verbally against it and
spoke openly in front of the females. The male
patrol officers also told their female colleagues
that "women do not belong on the streets." Thus,

the female uniformed officers in the Atlanta Police
Department receive few votes of confidence from male
peers or superior officers.

Although seldom partnered with either a male or
female (cars are mostly one-man), the women were frequently backed up on calls by males. The latter
often usurped the female officers' role and dominated the encounter. This was particularly true on
drunk or fight calls where the possibility of
violence was not remote. Some males even arrived
on a female's routine call, stood around for awhile
as if assessing the possibility of trouble, and then
left. The women's reactions to this male protective
attitude and behavior will be elaborated upon in
Chapter 8. The men's frequent presence and domina-
tion of the females' calls undoubtedly does affect
the latter's style of policing. In any case, it is
difficult to assess females' performance since they
are seldom permitted to act alone.

The present findings do concur with Sherman's
(1975) conclusion that women patrolling in suburban
St. Louis engaged in less preventive patrolling
activity. Although neither sex spent the prescribed
amount of time patrolling, the amount of their work
did vary by sex. The women did not actively try to
locate trouble spots. They cruised the main thoroughfares of their assigned beat. Most men drove
down alleys, through any housing projects on their
beat and often stopped the car near any group of
persons gathered in front of bars or shops. The
men seemed to also be more aware of traffic violators and quickly turned on the blue light and
chased the errant motorists. Females seldom used
their blue light or sirens, drove at a more sedate
pace, and rarely tried to find illegal traffic or
criminal activity. On emergency calls, it was rare
for a female officer to arrive first. This may be
due partly to their driving style.

At roll calls, at 59's, or on dinner breaks, one
often sees the uniformed males and females together.
The women are at least superficially accepted as
members of the group. The public also appeared to
accept the uniformed females as police officers but

the citizens' observed reactions in Atlanta were not as positive as other studies indicated (Milton 1972, 1974; Sichel et al 1977). Although overtly deferential to the females' authority, both male and female civilians usually turned to a male officer if one was present. Since the uniformed females were mostly as brief and unemotional as their male colleagues toward victims, it is doubtful that the female officers are regarded as more considerate and sympathetic. Due to their recent arrival on the street, the main reaction of the public to females patrolling appears to be curiosity. The women are frequently asked why they joined. Their departure from a call is occasionally accompanied by laughter; plus it is also not rare for civilians to point at uniformed women in a patrol car and laugh.

Few white officers, either male or female, were performing the prescribed duties in anything but a cursory manner. Their alienation from the hierarchy had been furthered by the recently promoted black sergeants, many of whom have been enforcing the rulebook much to the chagrin of officers who had developed a style of policing which included many infractions that had often been overlooked by the white brass. The result has been a token policing effort by the uniformed officers. Their remaining work time is spent in the personal pursuits outlined in the next chapter.

6

NONREGULATION ACTIVITIES

The purpose of this chapter is two-fold.
First, it will describe how the detectives and uniformed officers spend the hours of their shift when
they are not involved in policing duties. Secondly,
the broad range of rule infractions, which occasionally include actual illegal activities participated
in by some members of the bureau, will be discussed.
Thus, this chapter will present the final descrip-
tive data of the on-duty behavioral patterns of members of the police subculture.

These illicit activities, perhaps more than the
policing duties described in the last two chapters,
further solidify the group since shared knowledge
and/or participation in acts that transgress the
orders of the police hierarchy and in some instances
the law, create deeper ties of loyalty among officers. At this time in Atlanta, however, the "group"
has become two separate groups divided along racial
lines. The black officers who were observed did
commit many of the offenses outlined below, but seldom in concert with white officers. The data below
is therefore largely an account of the white segment of the department although in fact it may be
true for all police officers.

The radio calls received by a detective may
consume an hour of his watch. On many shifts, no
calls are received. Investigative work is done in
a perfunctory manner and can usually be completed
during one shift of the detective's work week. The
log in Chapter 4 has indicated that it is not
unusual for the hours of a watch to pass without any
police work conducted. On five shifts out of twenty-
two on Sex Crimes, six watches out of eighteen on
Homicide, and four out of eighteen on Robbery, the
detective(s) observed neither received any calls nor
conducted any investigative work. This occurred on
only one watch during the six months spent observing
Uniform. The uniformed officers handled an average
of six calls per shift with a range of zero to

twelve. The uniformed officer's hours are filled,
by necessity, with more police work. Time out of
service on calls ranges from one to six hours. The
norm is approximately two hours. Therefore, the
uniformed officer also has many hours left on each
shift when (s)he is supposed to be cruising the city
streets deterring crime, alert for criminal and
traffic offenders. Most white officers as discussed
in the last chapter do not, at this time, have the
"gung-ho" spirit that might inspire them to spend
their time at these tasks.

What then do the detectives and the patrol officers do? Every police recruit quickly learns the
meaning of a frequently used term in police jargon
that denotes the manner in which most of this free
time is spent: cracking. Although it is often employed to refer specifically to sleeping, the crack
or cracking may also refer to many different types
of places and activities. A main taxonomic distinc-
tion is between the indoor and the outdoor crack.

Indoor Crack

Many detectives, sometime during the shift,
head for their homes. It is not unusual for detectives to spend several hours at their houses eating
dinner, watching TV, or participating in other
domestic activities. The only restriction upon the
ability to crack at home is the distance from the
city of Atlanta: their radios must be able to receive and transmit, and they must be within a
reasonable distance for responding to a call. Very
few uniformed officers can go to their homes because they must remain within the boundaries of
their beats or an adjoining beat; and it is rare for
white members of the bureau to live within the city
limits. The patrol officers are further restricted
by their uniforms and marked vehicles. Thus, their
cracking must be conducted in a more surreptitious
manner. There are domiciles other than one's home
that are ideal for spending "city" time in. Both
detectives and uniformed officers may drop in at a
friend's home, in many cases a female friend—this
will be discussed further below.

A few detectives, either through police contacts or through extra job connections, have access
to certain hotels and motels in the Atlanta area.
This is an ideal set-up for some morning watch detectives who receive very few calls. The partners can
either take turns sleeping or, having developed an
internal alarm system which awakens them when a signal is directed to their squad, they can both sleep.
It is also not unknown to have female companionship
in these hotel cracks.

Almost every white uniformed officer has a particular indoor crack. These range from the city
morgue to a funeral home, gas station, liquor store,
convenience store, theater, and fire station. The
last are a common crack since firemen seemingly welcome their fellow city employees. The officer may
sit for several hours watching TV, chatting with the
firemen and occasionally sharing their home-cooked
dinners. There are times during a crack that an
officer becomes engrossed in a television program
and is then interrupted by a summons on the radio.
Irritable and muttering obscenities, (s)he proceeds
to the call and attempts to handle it as expedi-
tiously as possible in order to return to the television. Thus the indoor crack and its various
activities may assume an importance out of proportion to the presumed reality of policing.

Outdoor Cracks

Detectives, having access to all areas of the
city and outlying districts, are able to drive to
wholly deserted places far removed from the threat
of exposure. They may remain in the car for several
hours, particularly on morning watch, sleeping,
talking, or enjoying some female companionship.
Detectives generally feel more secure in the outdoor crack than indoors since there is less chance
of being informed on. Officers who have gone home
during working hours have occasionally been reported
to Internal Affairs by neighbors who have spotted
the detective car and presumably resent how their
tax money is being spent. The outdoor crack is
usually a shared experience by detective partners

and increases their feeling of togetherness whereas on indoor cracks the partners often separate and go to different sanctuaries.

Uniformed officers generally must be satisfied with alleys and the rear lots of abandoned buildings. The officers may read (comic books are not uncommon), do crossword puzzles, rest their eyes, or listen to transistor radios which are often carried to work against city policy. The solitary retreat may develop into a group 59 if the crack site is well known. However, many officers maintain an air of strict secrecy from all concerning the location of their private parking areas.

Other Activities

Trim refers to the women or girls on an officer's beat who are generally acknowledged as sexually available to police officers. Police officers, apparently by benefit of their uniform or the power implicit in their role, have a vast feminine following who pass from officer to officer. No male trim were observed. Since most female officers were socially involved with male police officers, they did not appear interested in making civilian conquests. The officers rate trim on a scale which varies from "tush hogs" (physically unattractive and whorish) to day watch trim, meaning a type of female with whom one would not mind being seen in the daylight.

Trim often drive around the zones in search of uniformed officers who may pull up alongside and converse with them at length. Afterward, the officers always speak of the girl in degrading terms, using the labels "pig" or "tramp." Officers also allegedly engage in sexual relations with trim at the latters' homes during working hours. This is made possible by the assistance of fellow officers who cover up the activity by handling any calls directed to the otherwise occupied officer. For example, if a signal is dispatched to car 3304 who is involved with a female, his friend in car 3305 will quickly inform the dispatcher that he is near the location and will handle the call.

Interestingly, almost every male interviewed disclaimed any personal involvement with trim although acknowledging the availability of girls and claiming that most of the other officers are indeed philandering with the zone trim.

Aside from the females labeled trim, there are other types of romantic partners encountered during working hours with whom the officers have more involved relationships.[1] In one classification are the mistresses of married officers, particularly detectives. Police officers do not appear to place a high value upon fidelity. Many detectives openly acknowledge their affairs. One could not say definitively how much of the talk is only braggadocio and how much is fact, but few officers express guilt or shame in reference to adultery. It appears to be considered as a normal part of marriage. Frequently, one detective partner drops the other at his mistress's home and spends almost the entire watch handling any calls alone. This act of generosity is reciprocated in kind by offering the other officer opportunities to visit his woman friend or his wife on another shift. Some detectives claim that it is mainly during on-duty hours that they are able to carry on their extramarital affair since many are employed at other jobs and do not have the "personal" time available. The promotion to detective seems to include a shift from the purely sexual relationship with trim at the uniform level to the development of a more long-term and deeper

---

[1]An interesting idea, told to me by several females who dated male officers, may bely the males' reporting of sexual activity. There may be an uncommonly high rate of impotency among police officers. The impotence reported seems to occur in relationships that involve emotional involvement. There is insufficient data to consider this as anything but speculation; however, since it seemingly does contradict the sexual activity norm among male officers, it should be mentioned.

relationship with a woman.

Another type of on-duty sexual relationship is between male and female police officers. The frequency of intra-police marriages will be shown in the next chapter. It is indeed no longer rare for male and female officers to marry, often following the divorce of one or both. These relationships are often initiated and developed during working hours. Uniformed officers assigned to the same zone have the best opportunity for meeting during the watch under secluded conditions if desired. If operating out of different parts of the city, ingenuity is required and meeting places such as the shop are found. Detectives or plainclothes officers are able to conduct an affair in more conventional settings such as one's home. Since several ex-partners have married it might be assumed that the close proximity of a detective car may sometimes promote romantic relationships.

Unmarried detectives and uniformed officers also may arrange to meet their girlfriends or fiancees during working hours. Occasionally, the police car may be used to convey the friend from a rendezvous to her home or elsewhere. The officer is then breaking two rules concurrently since civilians without authorization are not permitted to ride in city vehicles.

Aside from cracking and involvement in on-duty romantic relationships, police officers also engage in household and family-oriented activities while on duty. Shopping for gifts at holiday times and purchasing items for one's home or automobile are not uncommon although once again the uniformed officer approaches the stores with some trepidation, fearful that an irate citizen or an off-duty police officer working security might make a report to Internal Investigations. One female plainclothes officer was almost regularly able to pick up her child from elementary school and drive her home. Visits are made to family members and friends who are hospitalized in Atlanta, and officers occasionally drop in at parties on evening and morning watches.

Some officers, particularly those assigned to morning watch, become pranksters in order to occupy the quiet hours of the shift. Several detectives go to certain rat-infested areas and hold shooting contests, keeping track of the number of vermin killed by each participant with their service revolvers. This is a blatant infraction of local ordinances which control the discharging of firearms. Another favorite prank for some detectives and uniformed personnel is to drive along until an elderly black person, preferably carrying groceries, is spotted. The driver then backfires the police vehicle; the ideal consequence involves the nervous reaction of the victim who drops the groceries. One further caper should·be mentioned since it signifies the present alienation of officers from the administration. Several detectives drove into the police parking lot late at night and proceeded to remove most of the hubcaps from the city vehicles assigned to members of the ruling echelon--a small symbolic act of defiance.

The pranks and other personal activities that take place during working hours may be partly due to what some officers describe as the basic immaturity of almost every police officer. One officer said, "Being a cop is a way never to grow up. Cops are all kids just still playing cops and robbers."

Other Rule Infractions

The preceding sections outlined the major category of rule infractions committed by police officers: spending police time on personal activities. In addition, there are a plethora of rules broken by almost all officers. Several of these, such as lengthy 59's were mentioned in Chapter 5. The following is a brief summary of some of the offenses that were observed during the year of field work.[2]

One officer revealed that he carries a knife in his briefcase and believes that this is a fairly common practice among his colleagues. The purpose is to provide a legal rationalization for either physically abusing a suspect or for arresting a suspicious person by claiming that the weapon was on that person. Apparently weapons are not the only objects that have been planted on suspects or prisoners. Another officer carries a small quantity of marijuana to assure the arrest of persons whom he is certain are drug dealers although at the time of arrest they might not be in possession of a drug. The officers' reasoning in both instances for transgressing the law is that they are actually upholding the judicial system. Since the pendulum of justice, according to police officers, has shifted so far to the left-- protecting the accused and constraining the officers' former ability to coerce the "truth" from suspects-- these officers believe that they are merely attempting to equalize what has become a radicalized legal system.

Graft in Atlanta, according to detectives and uniformed officers, does exist in the higher levels of the police bureaucracy. No specific accusations are made but it is widely assumed that most of the "brass" receive "payoffs" from various businesses and/or syndicate operations. The Vice squads, Gambling, Prostitution, and Narcotics, are usually mentioned as assignments where it is easy to be "on the take." Aside from these areas, officers

---

[2]Since officers are extremely paranoid at this time, I was often undoubtedly not exposed to all of the deviant behavior. Fortunately, I was able to create a good degree of rapport with several officers whom I believe behaved as usual, flagrantly breaking rules in my presence.

disclaimed the existence of any graft or corruption.[3] The only acknowledged illegal acquisition of money was by uniformed officers who admit that if they come upon a corner dice or card game and the participants run away, the officer(s) pocket any money left on the ground.

Aside from currency, the widespread practice of accepting "freebies" and half-priced items may be considered a type of graft. The commissioner so defines it and has outlawed these practices, citing his view that acceptance of gratuities creates an indebtedness of police officers to the citizen gift-givers. Many officers do admit that if, for example, a restaurant owner who has provided half-priced meals for a length of time gives the officer a traffic citation to "take care of," it will usually be "fixed." They claim, however, that any major illegal activities would not be overlooked. The officers further feel that they are earning the free coffee or meal by their presence in the restaurant which presumably acts as a crime deterrent. Aside from food, officers are often able to develop relationships with certain shopkeepers on their beats that result in free or wholesale commodities such as cigarettes, liquor, and reading material. If one officer has a connection for a certain item, such as auto parts or baby food, (s)he often makes it known to friends in the department. Thus few

------

[3]I hesitated to question officers directly concerning graft for two reasons. Primarily I did not wish to increase their paranoia nor detract from any rapport I had developed. Secondly, I was warned early in the year not to ask any "sensitive" questions or my physical well-being might be jeopardized. Many researchers have discussed the "Code of Secrecy" which Beizel (1975: 144) states is acted out by police more than by any other professional group. Since some police officers have suffered indictment, conviction, and stiff prison sentences for as little as taking a few dollars from a proprietor, the Secrecy Code is strongly enforced.

officers must pay retail prices for many necessities and/or luxuries. Occasionally an officer is the surprised recipient of free goods or services merely by benefit of wearing a police uniform. For example, a female officer took a sofa cushion into a shop for repair on her way home from work. The proprietor refused payment, explaining that the officer in the area had always been kind to him and that he wanted to reciprocate. Entertainment is also often free for members of the bureau who can "badge" their way into movies, concerts, and athletic events either on or off duty. Fellow officers are frequently in charge of security at these entertainment centers and admit other officers without tickets.

Several officers used the presence of a female observer in the car in a role that overtly contributed to harassment but might be construed as entrapment. On one occasion the officer approached a male, known as an unlicensed peddler; he then turned to me and asked if this was the man who had sold me the watch. Before I could respond, the suspect confessed that he did sell watches and jewelry on the street, but he promised to stay out of that officer's beat. Presumably plainclothes females are also cast into similar roles on occasion--pretending to be the victim of various crimes. A male walking alone at night might be brought into the detective car where he is faced with a purported rape victim who is asked by the officers if "this is the man?"[4] As mentioned earlier, this is also a game frequently played with drunks.

Misuse of the radio in several ways by uniformed officers is a fairly common offense. Theoretically, only essential police-related information should be given over the radio with an effort at brevity in order to keep the radio open for emergency calls. In reality, officers often transmit non-police-related messages such as arranging

_____

[4]The use of the observer in these games might be construed as a test of attitude and loyalty to the police.

for meetings with fellow officers that are entirely
social in context. Nor is it unusual for a young
woman (trim) to ask an officer to put in a request
39 (information) at a certain location to another
car for her. Thus, the radio is used to facilitate
rendezvous.

In one zone, several officers who dislike both
the black sergeant and the female officer occasionally jam their radios when either begins to speak;
potentially a dangerous game that further dramatizes
the nonacceptance of some black superior officers
and some female officers.

Other rule infractions frequently committed
include using the blue light at nonregulation times
such as the end of the watch to hasten arrival at
the precinct or driving at excessive speeds without
a policing provocation. On one occasion, several
detectives decided to see what the maximum speed
capability of a new detective car was on an express-
way. A uniformed officer, not recognizing the city
vehicle as it sped by, began a chase which continued
for several minutes. The detectives were aware
that, since they were not en route to a call, they
would be in trouble if they were caught. They man-
aged to avoid the uniform vehicle by leaving the
highway, careening down local streets, and stopping
in a private driveway. The uniformed officer's
zone frequency had been monitoring the chase, tying
up the radio, and several uniform cars became involved. However, the detectives remained calm and
merely asked rhetorically, "What else can you do at
3:00 in the morning?"

One other practice should be mentioned, although its frequency could not be ascertained. Some
officers do drink alcohol on duty and/or shortly
before reporting to work. Trim are asked to buy
liquor for a uniformed officer and bring it to his
car. Some detectives, without the overt insignia
of their occupation, even drink in cocktail lounges
or restaurants during working hours. It is often a
solitary activity since one's partner or other colleagues may not approve. The disapproval stems
partly from the fact that officers must rely upon

129

the physical and mental astuteness of their co-workers; the use of alcohol may impede or impair the ability to fulfill this supportive role.

Other drugs, particularly amphetamines, are taken by some officers. "Uppers" may seem a necessity to officers working two jobs with little time for sleep. A few officers hinted that marijuana is smoked by some prior to work, but they were extremely hesitant about discussing its use. It is therefore not unlikely that on any given watch, several officers are either drinking, popping pills, or smoking pot--all activities which if discovered would mean immediate suspension.

It should now be fairly obvious that white male and female members of the Atlanta Bureau of Police Services break the monotony of police work with a wide assortment of deviant personal activities. Any officer whose behavior does not conform to this pattern is regarded as "green," a gung-ho rookie, and although not a social outcast, the one who observes the rules is never wholly accepted into the circle of the police group. Tenure on the streets does seem to be positively correlated with the amount of non-policing pursuits. Undoubtedly, the occupation, with its relative freedom of movement, has always involved some nonregulation activities by officers. However, the present political climate has increased the amount of deviance. Since white officers are rarely committed attitudinally to the prescribed duties, they fill in the hours with their own individual interests.

This is an area which has been neglected in other literature on policing; an absence which may be due to previous research techniques that did not permit the degree of familiarity and candor between the police and the researcher which is necessary for a complete depiction of police life. The non-policing aspect of the job has become an intrinsic part of the group structure, further alienating the police from both the public and the police hierarchy and further promoting the solidarity of comrades engaged in the same covert activities.

7

POLICE OFFICER PROFILE

This chapter, divided into three sections, includes data on both male and female officers. It
emphasizes the contrast between their attributes and
responses: therefore, responses will be separated
by sex. First, some data on the life history of the
sample will be presented; second, in an attempt to
obtain an insider's view of policing and the police
subculture, officers' responses to several open-
ended questions concerning their occupation are reported. The final section discusses conservatism,
found in other studies (Skolnick 1967; Rubinstein
1973) to be the main psychological trait common in
police officers. This study sought to verify this
conclusion first by asking the officers to identify
themselves on a conservative-liberal continuum and
then by asking their views on certain issues related
to law enforcement.

Life History

The average age of the informants is shown in
Table 7. It may appear surprising at first that
female officers are either older or the same age as
their male counterparts since their average tenure
in the department is only two and a half years as
compared to six years for male officers. The older
age of female recruits may be due to the fact that
many enter policing after having worked at other
jobs first. Their prior occupations ranged from
telephone operators to secretarial work and accounting. Also, as indicated in Table 8, females had
more education prior to joining the bureau. In comparison, many of the males entered policing either
directly after several years of college or after
serving in the military. The difference in tenure
of males and females may be significant in explaining some of the contrasts in their responses since
it was found that length of tenure as a police officer increased the degree of self-described conservatism.

Age Distribution of Interview Sample

	Mean Age
Female	
White	26.4
Black	29.3
Male	
White	27.8[a]
Black	26.5

Table 7

[a]For detectives--28.7; for uniformed offi-
cers--25.6.

Education of Interview Sample

	High School		Less than 4 years college		BA/BS		Post- Graduate	
	No.	%	No.	%	No.	%	No.	%
Female								
White	2	20	5	50	3	30	0	0
Black	0	0	2	66	1	33	0	0
Total	2	15	7	54	4	31	0	0
Male								
White	9	25	18	52	8	23	2	6
Black	0	0	2	100	0	0	0	0
Total	9	24	20	54	8	22	2	5
Total sample	11	22	27	54	12	24	2	4

Table 8

As Table 8 indicates, the stereotype of the uneducated cop is largely untrue. Almost one-fourth of the sample have university degrees, and more than one-half have completed some college. Of the latter, many are going to school concurrently with policing-- most majoring in criminal justice. As stated earlier, they are paid by L.E.A.A. to further their education and have the added incentive of a higher step salary for a college degree. Those who had degrees prior to entrance in the department specialized in a broad spectrum of subjects including criminal justice, political science, math, social work, and journalism. The educated officer does appear to be a fairly recent phenomena. Older informants had only completed high school.

It must be noted that the educational statistics presented here may not be exactly representative of the department as a whole. Unfortunately, the Atlanta Bureau of Police Services' personnel division has not produced a statistical breakdown of officers' educational level. However, as stated earlier, in several squads and zones (evening watch) almost every officer was either interviewed, ridden with, or known socially by the observer. As a group, their educational level did not deviate from the sample. It should also be noted again that superior officers did not select the more educated members of a squad or zone for the observer to ride with and interview. In almost every instance it was a matter of convenience; the researcher was placed with an officer who did not have a partner for the watch.[1] Therefore, based upon a familiarity with many members of the department who were not a part of the sample and based upon the relatively unstructured nature of my "partner" selection, Table 8 may be considered as fairly representative of the department as a whole.

---

[1] This should allay arguments that my sample was more educated than the norm since it might be falsely assumed that superiors arranged for me to ride with only the more educated and liberal officers.

Informants were asked which of nine socio-economic groups they had been raised in. The results are shown in Table 9. Most officers felt that they were brought up in one of the middle-class groupings, 88 percent of the entire sample. Further questions concerning family background revealed that only 2 percent of the officers had been raised to feel an identity with a particular ethnic group. However, a fourth of those questioned had been brought up as "white Southern Baptists." This religo-regional self-label was volunteered by the informants and not given as the response to a particular question.

The high incidence of divorce among police officers has frequently been discussed in the literature. As Table 10 shows, this is indeed true among Atlanta police officers: 42 percent of the sample had been divorced once. Based upon only those officers ever married, the percentage is of course higher, with fully one-half divorced at least once. It should be noted that the divorce rate among females exceeds that for male officers. Many of these divorces occurred after the women became police officers. Coinciding with this fact is the high incidence (almost one-half) of females in the sample now married to police officers. However, this figure applies only to white females. None of the black females interviewed were married to, or dated, fellow officers.

Most wives of police officers have jobs, presumably to maintain a fairly high standard of living exemplified by the purchase of new suburban homes by many white married males. Myth and some marriages perpetuate the idea that police officers often marry nurses since their shift hours coincide. However, the wives of the males interviewed worked in a broad variety of professions including nursing, policing, teaching, secretarial work, or as stewardesses, and insurance agents. Many of the men stated that they rarely see their wives since one or both are always working. This may be one factor accounting for the high divorce rate.

As the last chapter indicated, officers have

Socioeconomic Level of Interview Sample

	Upper Class						Middle Class						Lower Class					
	Upper		Middle		Lower		Upper		Middle		Lower		Upper		Middle		Lower	
	No.	%	No.	%	No.	%	No.	%	No.	%	No.	%	No.	%	No.	%	No.	%
Females	0	0	0	0	0	0	3	23	6	46	3	23	1	8	0	0	0	0
Males	0	0	0	0	1	3	10	27	10	27	12	32	2	5	1	3	1	3
Total	0	0	0	0	1	2	13	26	16	32	15	30	3	6	1	2	1	2

Table 9

Marital Status of Interview Sample

	Divorced		Divorced more than once		Married, never divorced		Single	
	No.	%	No.	%	No.	%	No.	%
Females	9	69	1	8	1	8	3	23
Males	12	33	2	5	21	56	4	11
Total sample	21	42	3	6	22	44	7	14

Table 10

ample opportunity during working hours to develop extramarital relationships. Presumably these occasionally lead to divorce when the infidelity is discovered or the officer wishes to marry his mistress. It should also be noted that police officers often do not feel able to relate to their non-police spouses. The feeling of alienation to the public may extend to the conjugal unit. It may also partly account for the high number of intrapolice marriages. (There are, however, some officers who have remained married for ten or more years, so apparently a stable marriage is possible for a certain percentage of officers.) Rubinstein (1973) summarizes the tension-producing forces of policing upon family life. He notes that there are many things that a police officer sees that he either cannot or prefers not to tell his spouse. The officer is away from home a great deal, and the wife knows that he has many opportunities to meet other women. Also, due to his hours and days of work, there are family occasions and holidays at which he is not present (Rubinstein 1973: 437-38).

Policing and the Occupational Subculture

The subject of how officers perceive themselves will be dealt with fully in the next chapter when self-image is discussed. The following section is concerned with the officers' recognition of membership in a group, somewhat alienated from the rest of society.

The informants were asked, "What is it like for you being a police officer?" The question was phrased in a rather ambiguous and open style in an attempt to elicit the major thoughts concerning the policing role in the officers' minds. As the comments below indicate, there was a marked similarity in the responses to such a broadly phrased question.

Females generally expressed more positive feelings about their occupation than their male counterparts:

My life has widened in many respects and

narrowed in many. I've seen more things and done more than most people will ever see. (white, plainclothes officer, age 24)

It's challenging and different. I like it and it's usually enjoyable. I look forward to going to work for the most part. (white, Uniform, age 26)

It's interesting. There's never a dull moment. Every now and then you get afraid of things. You're more attuned to danger and notice things more. (white, Uniform, age 24)

It doesn't conflict with my personal life. I like it. I like working with people. My only objection is that there's more of a tendency for men to make passes at you. (black, Uniform age 29)

The female officers frequently compared policing to their prior desk-type jobs, emphasizing the boring nature of the latter. Their pleasure in policing seems to stem mostly from the relative degree of flexibility and the potential excitement. Although no woman in the sample responded entirely negatively, the following responses do include a negative aspect:

It's discouraging most of the time. The main source of this is the courts. It's exhilarating but frustrating with many ups and downs that make it a difficult job to live with. (white, plainclothes age 28)

It's different things at different times. Frustrating, fun, frightening, irritating, and monotonous. (white, Uniform, age 24)

It varies at times. It's very good when you work under a supervisor who isn't

prejudiced against females. If you get
one who is, it can be hell. (white,
plainclothes, age 28)

It is noteworthy that only one female informant has mentioned her sex as a factor in her role
as a police officer. However, Chapter 8 will illustrate that all female officers are well aware of
their identity as female officers and the reaction
of male officers and the public to them.

A few males who were questioned about their perception of policing responded with entirely favorable sentiments:

It's not routine. It gives some feeling
of self satisfaction. I enjoy the job--
working with people. (white, Detective,
age 32)

I enjoy it, am dedicated to it. Anyone
here over five years is dedicated to it.
It's hard to leave. (white, Detective,
age 31)

However, most of the men expressed ambivalent feelings in their answers as the comments below show:

It's an exciting job; an extremely frustrating job; self-rewarding; a low paying
job. I feel restricted in the things I
can do in my personal life because of
possible repercussions from the police
department. (white, Detective, age 25)

It's satisfying and dissatisfying. It's
very rewarding knowing that you've accom-
plished something. And satisfying in knowing that you're performing a vital service
that everyone's not capable of performing
well. You need to be personable, able to
make decisions and be compassionate. But,
you bust your butt and people don't give
a damn. (white, Detective, age 31)

It's frustrating. The police department

has incompetent leadership and the
courts set everyone out on the street.
You can't get ahead. Have to know
someone. But it beats an eight to
five job. (white, Uniform, age 27)

The next responses represent a negative view that
appears to be partly the result of high expectations
concerning the job which the reality has proven to
be false:

It's not at all as I expected. A disappointment. I grew up always wanting
to be a cop and built up opinions about
it that aren't that way. It's fulfill-
ing to some extent--ups and downs.
(white, Uniform, age 28)

I had a feeling of wanting to do something. . .trying to make some changes,
helping people. But after eighteen
months, I've found it impossible.
(white, Uniform, age 23)

The key term in most responses was "frustration."
The officers often expressed the feeling that
neither the brass, the courts, nor the public is
backing them up.

Attitudes concerning the public were focused
upon in several questions. The first is tabulated
in Table 11. Almost all the officers polled believe
that the police officer in Atlanta is somewhat
alienated from non-police. This is certainly not a
new idea. Prior studies have emphasized the isolating effects of policing. For instance, one study
(Cumming, Cumming, Edell 1969) found that many officers were bitter about the punitive labels applied
to them in a world that values warmth, and that they
resented the ingratitude of the public. The researcher found this attitude reflected in a catch
phrase, "I hate citizens." Atlanta officers were
quite verbose in their answers to the question of
alienation although a yes or no could have sufficed.
Their responses below provide a deeper insight into
why police officers feel such a strong identity with

Alienation Between Police and Public

Is There a Sense of Alienation Between
Police and Public in Atlanta?

	Yes		No	
	No.	%	No.	%
Females	12	93	1	7
Males	36	97	1	3
Total sample	48	96	2	4

Table 11

their occupational group:

Females

> We live in a different world and have
> nothing in common with normal people.
> My neighbors don't understand me. I
> associate only with my own kind because
> they share my prejudices, cynicism, and
> mistrust. (white, plainclothes, age 28)

> There is definitely an in-group among
> police. People don't want to be cops.
> They don't like cops and they fear us.
> The officers feel that the public
> doesn't like them. All of this pro-
> duces separation. (white, plainclothes,
> age 28)

> It's not so much alienation as isolation.
> I'm not sure if it's the working hours
> or the environment, but there's a group
> coherence not found in other occupations.
> They seem to stress this in the police
> academy; that most of your friends will
> be police officers. (white, Uniform,
> age 30)

Males

> There's definitely alienation. Police
> officers are suspicious about just
> about everybody. People in general
> don't see the things we see. (white,
> Detective, age 30)

> Definitely. First of all no one likes
> to go to jail and the first impulse of
> a civilian when the police are around,
> on or off duty, is that they enjoy put-
> ting people in jail and are there for
> that. (white, Detective, age 36)

> Yes, and it will always be that way.
> It's a contrast between the haves and
> have nots--authority. (black, Detec-

143

tive, age 26)

Thus, paranoia on both sides, according to the officers, is a major factor in creating a wall of alienation between the police and the public. Police officers, constantly seeing the worst in human nature, admit that they tend to develop an extremely cynical and mistrustful view of man. Skolnick (1967) stated that the danger variable in policing makes officers suspicious, that they are trained to be suspicious and this acts to isolate them socially. The public, according to the police, mistrust police because they have authority and the potential power of arrest. Skolnick notes that the authority variable in the officers' role also tends to isolate them since they must enforce laws that represent a puritanical morality (e.g., involving drunks, drugs, and traffic).

Other studies have also emphasized the distinctive hours and days off as promoting friendship only with other officers and thus promoting an occupation isolation. Rubinstein's 1973 study of the Philadelphia police found that most officers only have police friends since an officer's relationship with non-police is limited by reticence on both sides. Philadelphia officers stated that if they became friendly with neighbors, someone eventually asked a favor which could not be granted or complained about the conduct of another police officer.

In light of these studies, the results presented in Table 12 are somewhat surprising. The officers in the sample have more civilian social acquaintances than police friends. Further questioning revealed that in most cases at least one-third of the civilian friends had been acquired since the informant became a police officer. The social contacts include work colleagues of spouses, fellow players at athletic events, and friendships originating from religious groups. The statistics may be misleading however since a large proportion of the informants stated that they have little time for friends and only see two or three people socially.

Friends of Police Officers[a]

What Percentage of Your Friends Are Police Officers? (Average responses of sample informants)	
Females	58
Males	38
Total sample	43

Table 12

[a]The term "friend" was defined as a person one saw socially outside of work. This definition was developed from the responses of key informants.

The range of responses is also interesting.
Only one of the thirteen female officers has 10 percent or fewer police friends as compared to thirteen
of the thirty-seven male informants. From interview
data, it appears that many female officers lost all
their civilian friends when they joined the force.
As one female said, "Everyone wanted to know why and
no one understood. They all stopped calling me."
Females also almost exclusively date male officers
and a high percentage are married to policemen.
Several unmarried female officers stated that they
do not tell non-police males whom they meet socially
that they are police officers because they believe
that this might deter any romantic involvement.

To further probe the question of alienation,
the informants were asked how they feel the public
views the police in Atlanta. Almost all of the
responses were strongly negative:

Females

> Some regard police with apprehension
> more than anything because each police
> officer's different and the public
> doesn't know what type you are. There
> are some who just don't like us; some
> who are very nice; some expect too
> much of you. (white, Uniform, age 28)

> Old ones take a pretty friendly outlook.
> Young ones consider us pigs because
> they fear interference with doping and
> other illegal activities. (white,
> Uniform, age 26)

> Rich whites think we should be out
> fighting crime, and please don't give
> me a ticket. Black females accept us
> better than black males. To black
> males and poor whites we are "honky
> motherf____." The majority do not
> like police. There are exceptions to
> all this. (white, Uniform, age 24)

> Blacks and whites have the same feeling.

146

Some look at us and think we're not
worth a flip. Some look at us like
we are a big farce . . . and sometimes
I wonder. (white, Uniform, age 24)

There's a segment of people that I
know from experience view police officers with a negative attitude--blacks
and a few young whites. The older
blacks grew up with a fear of the police
and the younger ones just don't respect
the law. The middle-class blacks view
the police officers as nothing--just
as little servants. Then there's a segment, mostly white, they look at the
Police Department; they don't think
much of this department primarily because of the administration. (black,
plainclothes, age 29)

Males

Generally most people view us as a
necessary evil. They want us to
catch the guy that ripped them off.
But they don't want to be bothered
with other things. (white, Detective,
age 29)

As unprofessional hardnosed rednecks.
(white, plainclothes, age 25)

The black community views the police
as an army of occupation trying to control their behavior; the business community as a tool to protect businesses;
the average middle-class as inefficient
but there for their benefit; and younger
people view us as a threat. (white,
Detective, age 27)

I think the public, all people who are
working class, resent authority, resent
being looked over by someone else. Our
low salary is a reflection of what the
public thinks of the police. When the
public notices you, you're either sit-

147

ting in a coffee house or speeding
through the street--they say, "Look
that's all he's good for." They
never see us at 2 a.m. going after a
burglar or a homicide detective at
the crime scene. They just see us as
a necessary evil. (white, Detective,
age 31)

They only care for the police when they
need them. The upper-class looks down,
we're their peasants. The lower-class
hate you because you enforce the law on
them. (white, Uniform, age 23)

They feel the policemen are as a general
rule mean and the only thing we want to
do is harass people and issue citations.
They think police are not really concerned with helping the public but more
interested in just the eight hour job
to make the money--no compassion.
(black, Uniform, age 27)

An interesting facet to the responses was the
almost universal tendency for the officers to separate the public into segments. Many informants expressed discomfort with the question and asked if
they could respond in sections. Officers answered
quickly and concisely. Judging by the complexity
of some responses it might be assumed that this is
a topic to which many officers have given much
thought.

A rather surprising fact that emerges from the
comments is the negative perception concerning the
white segment's attitudes about police. Labeled by
class, race, or occupation, most officers seemed
particularly upset when discussing the condescending
and patronizing attitude that they detect in interactions with the nonblack lower and middle classes.
National surveys of prestige have placed policing
quite low in status. In 1963, police officers were
ranked forty-seventh out of ninety occupations on a
prestige scale (Hahn 1974: 17). Thus, the indifference and superiority that officers sense from the

public may indeed be factually based.

This study was unable to include research into the public's attitude toward police. However, previous research has found that the policing role in the United States may be especially difficult. Patrick (1972) hypothesizes that this is due to a type of social order in which the principle of individual freedom is valued so highly. Patrick further states that the duties of police officers have never been clearly defined to the public who therefore visualize the frequent discharging of weapons and frequent arrest of offenders of major crimes, an erroneous image further perpetuated by the mass media. In any case, whether it is indeed fact or police paranoia, officers definitely do not feel appreciated or liked by any major segment of the Atlanta population. This attitude may not be universally held by American police. In fact, almost fifty percent of the Pittsburgh police felt that the general public respected and supported police officers (Scaglion 1973: 48).

Strong feelings of alienation, if not overt hostility, also emerged in the responses to the question, "How do you, as an officer, feel about the public in general?"

Females

> Some of them are O.K. but a lot of times, there are some that you can do without. I think it's their attitude to me. If I get good vibes, I give it back. (white, Uniform, age 24)

> I hate them all. (white, Uniform, age 24)

> Sometimes I get tired of the public for being so stupid and for having no reason to call the police. They should solve their problems themselves. Should use their own heads. (white, Uniform, age 26)

> Very naive and trusting. (white, plain-

clothes, age 28)

Some I feel disgust for; some I feel pity
for, some not at all. (black, Uniform,
age 29)

In general as being confused or ignorant
about police functions. I guess that's
basically why there's so many complaints.
They don't know that what the police
officer did was in his line of duty.
Also the public is too dependent on the
police department. I think that they
should be able to handle their own
children--domestic and social problems.
(black, Uniform, age 29)

Males

Uninformed and out of contact with
reality--propogandized. (white,
Detective, age 25)

Misinformed, apathetic, and generally
capable of anything the human mind
can perceive. A cut below animals.
The nature of man is money--do anything for money. (white, Detective,
age 27)

They're quick to criticize and rarely
thank you for a job well done.
They're not aware of the internal
affairs of the police department.
(white, Detective, age 28)

They show massive indifference to
everything. They don't want to get
involved in anything and they use
the police for their own convenience
and that's all they want, example,
to make reports for the insurance
companies. (white, Uniform, age 32)

They ought to get from me what they
pay for. It's a job to me. (black,

150

Detective, age 26)

The next response is atypically positive. The officer had an unusually strong, gung-ho attitude after
two years of policing.

> I just go out every day with a neutral
> attitude. I just pretty much like
> people. (white, Uniform, age 23)

The question was deliberately phrased in a broad
manner in order to see what aspect of the public
the officers are primarily concerned with. The
marked uniformity in responses, centering upon the
public's apathy and ignorance, and the officers'
general cynicism about mankind, is a further indication of the shared ethos resulting from common
experiences and membership in the police group.

Subsequent questions dealt with the officers'
feelings about victims and perpetrators. As shown
in their joking behavior following interactions with
victims, informants seldom expressed a concern for
victims. It was an almost universal consensus that
most victims contribute to the crimes by their
naivete and ignorance. Some do sympathize with the
victim vis-a-vis the courts. The officers' attitude
concerning children as victims of child abuse,
neglect, or molestation is strongly sympathetic.
Most officers become quite emotional when discussing
crimes against children, often stating that that
would be one perpetrator whom they would gladly beat
up. Not surprisingly no one expressed positive
feelings for perpetrators. Most comments centered
upon the idea that perpetrators should receive
tougher sentences and not get off on legal techni-
calities.

Other Related Issues

The homogeneity of attitudes found in the previous section extends to topics only indirectly
related to policing. Contrary to Skolnick's (1967)
conjectures, however, as Table 13 indicates, only
one-half of the officers questioned labeled their

Ideological Identification of Interview Sample

	Conservative		Liberal		In-between		Changed Since Joining Bureau	
	No.	%	No.	%	No.	%	No.	%
Females	4	30	0	0	9	70	8	62
Males	22	60	2	5	13	33	25	68
Total sample	26	52	2	4	22	44	33	66

Table 13

general orientation to life as conservative. Females
appear to be slightly less conservative, although
this may be due to their relative brevity of tenure:
63 percent of males with more than three years of
experience identified themselves as conservative,
compared to only 50 percent of the males with less
than three years experience. Education is also a
factor. Only 25 percent of the females and 50 percent of the males with college degrees considered
themselves to be conservative. An important insight provided by Table 13 is the fact that two-
thirds of the sample believe that they have changed ·
their general orientation to life since becoming
police officers. The shift is mostly from liberal
to in-between or conservative. Several officers
feel that they have changed from in-between to
conservative. Not surprisingly there were no shifts
toward liberalism. Thus, it appears that membership
in an occupational group can affect many of one's
attitudes and one's self image. Other researchers
have speculated that the high incidence of conservatism among police may reflect the type of person who
joins a police department. However, only 16 percent
of the sample felt that they had been conservative
prior to policing, and a surprisingly high number
identified themselves as ex-liberals.

The terms conservative and liberal were not
defined by the interviewer. The officers' responses
to the questions below seem to indicate a much
higher degree of conservatism (at least in issues
related to law enforcement) than identified by the
officers themselves. Therefore the above data can
be considered only as the informants' self-image,
not as an objective evaluation. It is still important, however, since it represents the officers'
emic view of themselves and their occupation.

When asked whether they favor capital punish--
ment, 100 percent of the males and 85 percent of the
females responded affirmatively. Of the entire sample, 96 percent advocated capital punishment for a
variety of crimes including murder (usually nondomestic), rape, robbery, and child-victim crimes.
The reasons for this belief in a "life for a life"
become apparent in the loquacious responses to

questions about the judicial and penal systems.
Most officers feel that the courts' life sentences,
when complemented with plea bargaining and "good
time," often result in convicted murderers spending
only a few years behind bars. Officers further
believe that the present prison system is failing
to rehabilitate, thus releasing felons who will continue to commit crimes. Thus officers state that
only death will remove the problem from society (and
the police).

The females' and males' opinions concerning the
courts and the prison system were markedly similar,
all stressing the negative aspects while often
suggesting theoretical models for improvement. Even
the terminology used was remarkably the same. "It
stinks," and "it's a joke," were frequently the intro-
ductory phrases to lengthy tirades that included
comments on corruption in the courts, legal games,
failure of prisons to rehabilitate; the phrase
"country club" was often used to describe prisons.
The officers became more emotional and heated in
responding to these questions than at any other
time in the lengthy interviews. The responses below
indicate the deep concerns of the police about what
they feel are inadequate courts and prisons.

Question: "What do you think of the judicial system?"

Females

I'm more down on it than anything else.
My contacts with the court system have
been a farce. Superior court is less
farcical but I'm angry at them too because they are too lenient. Criminal
court is ridiculous. The solicitors
and prosecutors just don't know what's
going on. They haven't even briefed
them because there are too many cases.
(white, plainclothes, age 24)

It needs reforms. The courts are overcrowded with an emphasis on technicalities--
makes it a very slow process. There are
also dishonest judges and too much plea

154

bargaining. (white, Uniform, age 23)

I think it sucks. I had a case last
August that has been reset six times.
I have some I've never heard anything
about. Fines are too lenient. For
instance, with DUI's judges just give
fines to repeaters. The municipal court
judges set everybody loose just because
the police officer is not an eye witness.
The court system is too lenient. (white,
Uniform, age 24)

The courts are overcrowded so it's very
slow. The DA's and assistant DA's are
very impressive people although they may
appear unfeeling. The whole system is
going about as fast as it can. (black,
Detective, age 30)

Males

It's ridiculous because of the ABA
(American Bar Association). They condone disruption of court rooms and
delays. The lawyers put cases off to
get money. The lawyers and the judges
are drinking buddies. Where's the swift
trial? There are too many laws on the
books. It should be streamlined. The
DA's office has a lot of deadwood, and
police officers don't go over there.
The whole system is inefficient. The
whole thing is just geared to get lawyers
fees. (white, Uniform, age 32)

When a man is sentenced to five years he
should serve it. The judicial system is
weak. There are a lot of judges who hand
out sentences based upon political motivation (ambition). There are too many
cases that receive probated sentences.
And plea bargaining is a cop-out because
the DA's don't want to have a jury trial
in some cases where they should. And the
grand jury system should be eliminated.

155

It could be handled in municipal court
because they never have time to investigate. It would save money. (white,
Detective, age 25)

The pendulum of justice has fallen so
far to the rights of the accused that
it is denying the victims' rights.
Society is not getting the protection
it deserves. There is very little justice. The very rich and the very poor
get off; the poor because it's a very
paternalistic system and they're not
held responsible. We've got some crooked
judges; most try to do an honest job
though. (white, Detective, age 32)

The law right now encourages murder. A
man serves five years for armed robbery
vs. seven years for murder--and there's
less chance of getting caught if the man
is dead. With concurrent sentences, it
encourages multiple crimes. (white,
Detective, age 33)

It stinks. There's no unification in the
criminal justice system. Two people commit the same crime; one may receive fifteen years, the other ten, which is a big
inequality in sentencing. Should have
uniform sentences. Also the Supreme Court
has given too many rights to the criminals.
This has tied the police officers' hands.
We arrest "X" and have to protect his
rights. They get off on legal technical-
ities, not on guilt or innocence. (white,
Detective, age 28)

Judges have been criticized as too lenient
but we, the people, are the courts. Judges
can be voted out. If the judicial system
is failing, it is because we are failing.
(black, Detective, age 26)

Thus most police officers are dissatisfied with the
courts since the judicial system is contributing to

the frustration of policing. White police officers, feeling constrained from start to finish, have lost the incentive to make arrests. Legal decisions have curbed their previous techniques of obtaining confessions and other pertinent information. Even if they are able to build a "good" case, it is frequently bargained down, dismissed on a technicality, or, according to some officers, handled by a corrupt judge who utilizes his discretion in sentencing. Several officers expressed concern with what they perceive as reverse discrimination in sentencing: they believe that black offenders are receiving lighter sentences as a result of government pressure. Many officers also consider money to be a prime factor in obtaining acquittals or reduced sentences. Finally, the officers question their own usefulness when a perpetrator receives a lengthy sentence but is released after serving only one-third time.

The officers' knowledge of, and contempt for, the power of judges and plea bargaining contradicts to some extent the theories of Blumberg (1969) who stated that the court is a genuinely closed community that successfully conceals the true nature of its operations from the view of outsiders by socializing even the accusers (police officers) toward specific objectives of the court that are not part of the official goals of justice and due process. The comments above indicate, however, that the officers are quite dissatisfied with the steps that follow an arrest. It should be noted however that the sentiments of the black officers deviated from those expressed by white officers. Although unfortunately the number of black officers interviewed does not represent a large enough percentage of the whole to generate hypotheses, the black officers' responses were less hostile toward the judicial system.

Questioned about their attitudes on the penal system, most officers favored a combined punitive rehabilitation system and condemned rehabilitation programs that they feel have been proven inadequate by the high rate of recidivism. It is another issue that officers have apparently thought about, and their responses include their own models of the ideal penal system, models which appear to be based upon common criteria:

Females

Before I was a police officer, I felt
that the purpose of prisons should be
rehabilitation. But now I've seen that
there's hardly any rehabilitation.
Should depend on the crime. The physical
facilities need to be improved, to be ex-
panded. On the whole, it hurts society
so we need more and larger prisons to
punish. (white, plainclothes, age 24)

I think it stinks. They say they're over-
loaded and must put them back on the
streets. Should be rehabilitation, get
their warped minds cleared up. Now, it's
doing nothing. Just turning them right
out loose to do the same thing again.
(white, Uniform, age 27)

I think it's lousy. The state of Georgia
has the worst prisons. They get sentences,
serve a third with probation, and go right
back and do it again. (black, Uniform,
age 29)

They're overcrowded, and well, they're not
succeeding in their goal, rehabilitation.
Rehabilitation or punishment should depend
on the crime. Violent or persistent criminals should get punishment. (black, plainclothes, age 29)

Males

There should be dual standards. First
offenders should be given every opportunity in prison. Repeaters should just
be locked up. They can't respond to
punishment and the fear of jail doesn't
deter them. For the "pros" going to jail
is an occupational hazard. (white,
Detective, age 29)

I'd like to see first offenders get true
planned programs of rehabilitation; second
offenders more supervised rehabilitation;
third offenders just put in jail for the
protection of society. Today it's a bas-
tardization of both punishment and rehabilitation! A mixing together of all sorts of
criminals. (white, Detective, age 32)

The prison system is a farce. Every cell
has a color TV. The rehabilitation concept has proved to be a failure. We should
go back to the old punishment theory.
(white, Detective, age 25)

It stinks; too country clubish. They ought
to have to work, learn a trade, but no
color TV's. Should be a little bit of both
punishment and rehabilitation. (white,
Detective, age 25)

It's inadequate. I believe first felon
offenders should be given probation;
second offenders a short prison sentence
followed by parole; third-time offenders
should automatically get life without
parole. Today the main problem is mis-
management. People are put into prison
for a time period that's often changed
by parole. Rehabilitation programs are
funded by the government and by others.
The funds are cut off in the middle of a
program because it's not as effective as
expected. They don't give it a chance
to get rolling and get the bugs out of it.
(white, Uniform, age 24)

Thus, both white and black officers openly express
their view of the ineffectiveness of the prison
system. Recidivism is a major concern to police
officers who have been faced with an offender whom
they arrested, saw convicted, released from prison,
and arrested again.

The profile that emerges from this chapter is

of a male or female, in their mid-twenties, with
some college education, from a middle-class background, and with a 50 percent chance of being
divorced. The females are, on the average, slightly
older, better educated, and more likely to have been
divorced. The average officer feels alienated from
non-police but maintains social contacts with civilians. (S)he usually feels misunderstood, exploited,
and/or hated by the public and reciprocates with an
equally negative attitude toward the citizenry,
labeling the public as naive, ignorant, and/or apathetic. The Atlanta officers' responses do support
prior theories concerning the cynicism and isola-
tionism of the policing occupation. An overwhelming
96 percent of the officers polled stated that there
is alienation between the police and public in
Atlanta. Many officers find it difficult to shed
their occupational role when not at work, perhaps
contributing to the high incidence of divorce and
the frequency of endogamous marriages that have
occurred since women assumed active roles in the
bureau. Membership in the alienated police subculture also tends to promote a shared world view
that may be labeled conservative. The officers'
homogeneity in attitudes on three issues has been
illustrated: capital punishment, the judicial system, and the penal system. Significantly, most
officers feel that they have revised their opinions
since becoming police officers. Therefore the
shared social organization and the shared policing
and non-policing duties described in earlier chapters appear to contribute to, or result in, shared
attitudes toward the outside groups which substan-
tiate the delineation of a police subculture. The
marked similarity of the females' and males'
responses indicates the women's acculturation into
the ethos of the group. Their answers to open-
ended questions concerning the public and legal
issues were, in most cases, as negative and pro-
police as the males' sentiments.

FEMALES IN POLICING--THE INSIDERS' VIEWS

The last chapter has indicated that female officers' opinions on various topics tend to conform quite closely to those of their male counterparts. Does their expressed conservatism on certain issues, their sense of alienation from non-police, and their negative view of the public indicate that they consider themselves to be the equals of the male officers? This chapter will examine the question of females' acceptance into the close-knit police community and any effect that they have had on relations between the police and the public as discerned by the officers. My own observations and conclusions concerning women in policing will be summarized in the following chapter.

Female officers were asked whether they feel that being a police officer is the same for them as it is for males. A significant percentage, 85 percent, stated that their self-image or role is not the same.

> Most males regard their job in a different light than most females. For the men, the job is everything. The female has other things--responsibilities. (white, plainclothes, age 24)

> It's probably different. He probably thinks he's a macho he-man type whereas I don't think I present a masculine image. (white, Uniform, age 26)

> No, I think a lot of guys see it as a macho thing--he-man. For me, it's a job. (white, Uniform, age 24)

> No, it's a different image for me than for males. I enjoy this job because I like to be outside and with the public. The men see it more as a power thing.

(white, Uniform, age 27)

It differs in that I look at it as an
eight-hour job. Men look at it as full-
time. I'm a lady first, police officer
next. Men are just totally police officers. (black, plainclothes, age 29)

Therefore most women do not appear to regard themselves as female facsimiles of the male officer;
they emphasize the men's macho self-image and
their presumed total preoccupation with the job.

Table 14 confirms the idea that females do
not generally regard policing as a twenty-four-
hour-a-day job. However, the data does contradict
the women's assertion that all male officers think
of their job this way. The informants were asked
whether policing is a twenty-four-hour-a-day job
for them. The interviewer elaborated by defining
"twenty-four-hours-a-day" as the inability to ever
cast off the role or identity of police officer.
There is a marked difference in the responses between sexes, yet barely one-half of the male informants stated that policing is a totally encom-
passing occupation. Many of the males who
responded "no" added that it had once been a
twenty-four-hour-a-day job but that because of
their antipathy to the present administration,
they are determined to view it as "only" a job.

Several informants who answered "yes" expressed the attitude that it is others--neighbors and
friends, who reinforce their role as police officer during off-duty hours by seeking legal assistance from them, by complaining about other officers to them, or by behaving paranoiacly when they
are around. Apparently the difficulty of casting
off the role is greater for males. Most women
stated that they are women first and hence have
little trouble resuming their feminine civilian
role after leaving work.

Female officers were asked whether most of
their policing experiences with male officers have
been positive or negative. Most responses, as

162

Role Identity

Is Policing a Twenty-four-hour-a-day Job for You?

	Yes		No	
	No.	%	No.	%
Females	2	15	11	85
Males	20	54	17	46

Table 14

indicated below, were a mixture of favorable and unfavorable experiences and impressions:

> For me, it's been positive. We get along really well. They're all like my big brothers. The only trouble I've ever had was with a superior officer who'd often say, "I hate female officers!" (white, Uniform, age 27)

> Have a lot of kidding. No harassing situations. I take a lot of verbal abuse--typical male sexual insinuations. (white, plainclothes, age 24)

Sexual teasing is indeed an extremely common occurrence which has begun to infuriate some females who resent the incessant joking and the lack of seriousness in their interactions with males. Initially flattering, according to one woman who has contemplated leaving the department, it becomes frustrating when one's attempts to perform professionally are almost constantly responded to by levity and a flirtatious attitude.

> It's been neutral. It's sort of like they feel if they ignore me, I'll go away, like something bad they ate for dinner. I've not been treated badly here (zone) so far, just as one of the guys. But I've seen with other women-- they're tolerated, that's it. The first line men always say is, "I think women have a place on the police department but not on the streets. (white, Uniform, age 24)

The latter phrase "women do not belong on the streets" is frequently heard in conversations among males and in front of female officers. And as the following comments indicate, many women are aware of the negative or at least ambivalent feelings that the men have concerning women in policing.

Over here (Grady Hospital) there's
been no trouble. It's always seemed
like I've been wanted. They've
seemed to enjoy working with me. But
at school one of the instructors said
that women should stay home having
babies. And some have told me women
should be secretaries, nothing else.
Another said to me that if it was up
to him, he wouldn't have any females
in the department. A lot of men (especially the older guys) don't like
women in police work. (white, Uniform,
age 24)

It depends on the female herself. When
I first came down here it was mostly
negative due to the image I was present-
ing. Since I changed a lot (happily
married to a police officer and not
looking for anything) there's been no
making passes; friend to friend.
(white, plainclothes, age 28)

Males were skeptical when women first
came in because they felt that they'd
have to stop a lot of things like cus-
sing. But now they think of women as
partners. I told them I wasn't here
to change their ways. It's been in-
between. I don't like it when men talk
about other women, and a lot do. It
hasn't been bad. (black, plainclothes,
age 30)

Both. A third positive; two-thirds
negative. It's the way that they view
you--just as a woman. It seems as
though superior officers go from one
extreme to the other. They either have
no confidence in you and shield you,
e.g., always put you in a car with a
male officer; or they try to put you
on the spot. For example, I know some
cases where female officers were assigned
to morning watch in a very rough beat

alone. (black, plainclothes, age 29)

Thus most females admit that they have not been
accepted by males. Yet some responses showed an
optimism which may be unwarranted judging by the
feelings of males expressed below.

Female officers were asked whether they feel
that their presence in the department has affected
the self-images of male officers. The few affirmative responses were nonspecific, citing only a
belief that some changes in the males probably have
occurred. However, 85 percent responded that they
have not changed the way males regard themselves.
The responses below explain why:

> Not right now. There are too few women
> for one thing. Women are blending in
> with males and are not a separate group
> because women have handled themselves
> as well. (white, plainclothes, age 25)

The opinion above, expressed by a woman married to
a detective in the department, is atypical because it emphasizes the assimilation of females
into the police subculture. The other informants
stressed the opposite idea: males have not changed
because women have not been sufficiently accepted
into the group to be able to effectuate any impact
on male self-image:

> No, we haven't affected them in the
> least. They're so wrapped up in a
> macho image. (white, Uniform, age 24)

> No, because they still think that women
> can't handle it. They may be right.
> (white, Uniform, age 24)

> Don't think it's changed males because
> they're holding onto their image. They
> don't give females credit. You're not
> viewed as a police officer but as a
> policewoman. (white, plainclothes, age
> 30)

166

It's stayed the same because they look
at us as inferior and most don't think
we should be here. They say we get
soft jobs and don't do work the way
they do. (black, plainclothes, age 29)

A large percentage of females therefore do not
believe that they hold self-images similar to those
of male officers, and most do not feel that they
have affected the latters' view of themselves as
police officers. Furthermore, most females do not
believe that they have been accepted as equals by
the men in the department.

Table 15 can be interpreted as a summation of
the females' attitudes about themselves and their
professional relationship to male officers. Not
one female preferred a partner of the same sex. In
fact, a higher percentage of men said that they
have no preference or that it would depend upon the
beat and the individual female. Most of the women
expressed a greater trust in the policing capabilities of the males: "I'd feel safer." A few females
desired a male partner because they believe that
some situations arise for which a man is better
equipped due to greater appearance of physical
strength while other incidents are presumably better suited for a female. The other reason given
by some females for preferring male partners was
that they get along better with men, and stated
that most women are competitive and catty.

The reasoning behind the males' overwhelming
preferance for men partners will become apparent
below in their responses concerning female officers.
Male informants were initially asked whether they
considered their experiences with females to have
been positive or negative. Most officers expound-
ed at length upon their view of females in police
work. Officers were also asked the number of
policing experiences they have shared with women,
e.g., as partners or in backup. No positive cor-
relation was found between experience and specific
attitude except that the uniformed officers working in one particular zone, with two well-liked
white female officers, spoke more positively about

Partner Preference by Sex

	Prefer Males No.	%	Prefer Females No.	%	No Preference No.	%	Depends No.	%
Females	12	93	0	0	1	8	0	0
Males	30	81	0	0	4	11	3	8
Total sample	42	84	0	0	5	10	3	6

Table 15

the role of women in Uniform patrol:

> My feeling about females has changed
> for the better. I have found a lot
> of women on calls who are just apa-
> thetic and do the minimum amount of
> work like a lot of men too. There
> are also fairly aggressive female
> officers. They'll take bad calls and
> not request backup. (white, Uniform,
> age 23)

> I used to feel totally negative.
> Thought that they were incompetent.
> But after working with some, there
> are some women, a few, who are cap-
> able of handling the job and are
> even competent and have a lot of
> common sense. (white, Detective,
> age 32)

Their positive remarks were, however, directed more
towards specific individuals and do not include approval of most females in policing.

As mentioned earlier, the idea that females do
not belong on the street is frequently voiced by
the men as indicated in the following:

> They are effective as police in some
> fields such as Sex Crimes. But they
> aren't as effective on the beat because
> they can't get as close to the people
> as the male police officer. When
> you're a victim of a crime, you want
> an authority figure and people are
> leery about females. (white, Detec-
> tive, age 31)

> Most of the ones I've met honestly and
> sincerely try to do a good job but they
> just don't belong on the street. Most,
> because of their emotional background,
> are too unstable in high pressure situa-
> tions . . . there are exceptions to
> every rule. (white, Uniform, age 23)

169

It should be noted that neither of the above statements is directed against a particular female; the
informants are describing the female sex in general.
Other attributes ascribed to the sex en masse include a presumed ability to be more easily conned
by victims and perpetrators and a less imposing and
dominating physical presence.

Several officers who have been partnered with
females feel that the women's presence in the car
has an effect upon the males' policing performance:

> I'm not as aggressive when she's with
> me--chivalry or chauvinism. (white,
> Detective, age 29)

> It's very difficult. I've seen some
> who can carry the badge, have ability,
> and others who don't. Men, especially
> Southern men, are so used to treating
> women as something special. I think
> that the male officers are protecting
> the females. (white, Uniform, age 27)

The idea that females do not perform equally with
males in part because of the men's overprotectiveness and gallant attitude is exemplified in Tables
16-17. It is significant that 82 percent of the
uniformed officers, those men actually working on
the streets with women, stated that the males provide more backup for females while only 40 percent
of the male detectives believe this to be true.
The uniformed officers' responses are based upon
actual experience; in many cases the detectives
were merely echoing sentiments that flourish in
the police grapevine. Uniformed males further
believe that there is little need for female officers to call for backup since the men automatically
come to any call that is potentially dangerous.
"I think men make more of an effort to protect
them" (white male).

Some females, as the comment below indicates,
have felt frustration and dissatisfaction with
their constant male bodyguard:

Frequency of Calls for Backup

Do Women Call for Backup More Often Than Men?						
	Yes		No		No Opinion[a]	
	No.	%	No.	%	No.	%
Females	2	15	4	31	7	54
Males	11	30	16	43	10	27
Male Detectives	8	40	4	20	8	40
Male Uniform	3	18	12	70	2	12

Do Men Backup More for Women?						
	Yes		No		No Opinion	
	No.	%	No.	%	No.	%
Females	6	46	1	8	6	46
Males	22	60	3	8	12	32
Male Detective	8	40	2	10	10	50
Male Uniform	14	82	1	6	2	12

Table 16

[a]The high percentage of no opinions is due to high number of informants who had never been on the street.

Backup Dispatched by Radio

Does Radio Dispatch Backup More Often for Women?						
	Yes		No		No Opinion	
	No.	%	No.	%	No.	%
Females	7	54	0	0	6	46
Males	9	24	5	14	23	62
Male Detectives	4	20	1	5	15	75
Male Uniform	5	30	4	24	8	46

Table 17

When I was on the streets in 1973 there
were only two females in the zone and
it was true then. The sergeant might
be sitting outside waiting when I got
out of a call and in some cases the umbrella car was sent instead of me. I
didn't appreciate the men trying to
beat us to the call. (black, plainclothes, age 29)

Another woman, not in the sample, said that her
resentment of men accompanying her on calls reached
a point where she finally told them all to stop and
treat her just like a male.

Other women have opposite views, voicing appreciation of all the backup that they get:

Yes, males do. It's protection and I
don't resent it. I feel that they're
my buddies--we're friends. (white,
Uniform, age 29)

The range of females' responses to male backup are
exemplified in the different reactions the following male officer has received from the females
whom he admittedly backs up more often than the
men in his zone:

One woman said she had no intention of
having her ass whipped, of being a real
police, and stated that she expected
not to be because a male would always
be there. Another woman got mad at me
for backing her up on a "6" (burglary
in progress) although I would have for
a male too. She doesn't get backup now
because she doesn't want it. A third
woman will call a superior officer to
come to her calls. (white, Uniform,
age 24)

Another realm of male overprotectiveness is
perceived by females--radio dispatchers who either
assign calls in a female's beat to the umbrella
car or direct other cars to backup females in

situations where a male would not be dispatched to support another male. Table 17 indicates that more than one-half of the females polled believe that radio does not operate in an entirely equal fashion regarding the sexes.

The need to protect females was an almost universal complaint made by male officers. Many officers also voiced other negative comments--for example, that females enter police work for the money whereas the average male officer has more meaningful incentives and is more emotionally involed in the job:

> No, I don't believe that there's a place for women in the police department; from observation-their reservation in an actual frontline confrontation. "I'm only here for the check every two weeks" attitude. THEY'RE A CIVILIAN IN UNIFORM. (white, Uniform, age 23)

Another complaint stems from both the not infrequent placement of female recruits directly into plainclothes or in-house positions and the recent promotion of females:

> . . . and I don't agree with women using their bodies, sex, to get promotions. Automatically a woman knows that if she wants a man to do anything, she can somehow get what she wants. (white male, Uniform, age 24)

In order to further understand the reasoning behind the conviction of most males that women cannot perform adequately on the street, informants were asked questions based upon explanations for female inadequacy given during several preliminary interviews. The reasons given by these informants for the unacceptability of females on the street included (1) females' lack of physical strength; (2) females' presumed reliance upon their revolvers; (3) a presumed differential arrest rate, lower for female officers; and (4) the jealousy of male officers' wives. Only the first complaint found widespread agreement among the males in the research sample.

When asked how important physical strength is for a police officer, almost all informants immediately divided police into two groups, detectives and uniformed officers, stressing the latter's greater need for physical fitness. Several informants stated that it is not the strength itself that is important but rather the appearance of the officer and his (but not her) physical presence which can act as a deterrent to aggressive behavior. Most men admitted that violent encounters are rare, but added that on the occasions when physical strength is needed, females are not adequate. Female informants, acknowledging their relative lack of physical strength, stressed the rarity of incidents which require its use. One woman added that when a violent encounter does occur, male support is always there. Most females believe that their very lack of strength requires them to employ other strategies, more psychological and verbal, which may in fact be better than the show and utilization of brute force.

Many males also stated that given the females' lesser amount of strength, they may use their revolvers in situations where men would use physical force. Most officers did admit that this idea is not based upon actual observation but upon incidents which have become a part of the police lore. The cases involve a female officer shooting a perpetrator who in previous arrests had been taken into custody without the use of guns. Such accounts suggest that a male might not have had to use his weapon in a similar situation merely by virtue of the strong, masculine image he presented. When asked about specific policing experiences with females, however, only one officer claimed to have actually observed a woman drawing her pistol under circumstances which he did not believe merited it. Fifteen percent of the females polled feel that they, or other women, do use their revolvers more frequently than males. However, the majority expressed a nervousness concerning their revolvers and stated that they would only draw it as a last resort.

According to the bureau, officers' arrest
rates do not differ markedly by sex. Informants
universally agreed that arrest rates are not
accurate indices of police performance since different beats and different styles of policing
result in differential rates. Many males did add,
however, that they do not believe that females
show as much initiative in policing as males.
These assertions were accompanied by the males'
observations that women officers fail to patrol
high-risk areas, proceed slowly to dangerous calls,
and do not show the aggressive style of policing
that the men feel results in arrests.

The presumed jealousy of male officers' wives
was cited in preinterviews as a cause of the males'
resentment of female officers. Most married officers do concur that their wives have expressed
jealousy, apparently not without reason in some
cases.

> Yes, I've experienced my wife's jealousy.
> It's unbelievable. There's not as much
> going on as the grapevine says, but it
> is there. (white, Detective, age 32)

> Yes, my wife has said that the only rea-
> son women go into the police department
> is to be near men. (white, Detective,
> age 29)

Spouses' resentments of females who work with
their husbands does appear to exist. Whether this
has influenced the males' attitude toward women in
policing is a matter of conjecture. No male informant directly connected his negative attitude toward female officers to the jealousy of his wife.
Lack of physical strength appears to be the only
commonly shared reason why most men believe females should not be in uniform on the street.

Male informants were asked whether they feel
that having women working in all facets of police
work has affected their self-image as police

176

officers. The purpose of the question was to probe the acceptance or rejection of females into the police subculture. If entirely accepted, one would expect one of two responses: (1) that the males' self-image has remained the same since females have blended right into the image ("No change because police officers, male or female, have the same job to do and if they do it the same, it shouldn't influence the image"--white male, Detective, age 25); or (2) that their self-image has changed because females have been accepted into the group to the degree that their style has initiated changes in males' style or self-perception ("Yes, they've changed my self-image by showing me that what was my previous conception of being a police officer was not necessarily true"-- white male, Uniform, age 27).

However, most males believe that the presence of females has not affected them because the women are not viewed as police by them:

No, because I still believe it's a man's job. (white, Detective, age 28)

No, because most of the women here don't do their jobs. (white, Uniform, age 23)

A few males said that female officers have detrimentally affected their own feelings about being police officers because women have lowered the esteem and prestige of policing. But the vast majority of males denied that any changes have occurred, emphasizing in their responses the nonacceptance of females as police. Traditional stereotypes of the female sex as nonaggressive and nonauthoritarian are perceived by male officers as a threat to the long-standing masculine, macho image of police work. The very nature of the possible consequences of employing women, such as making a department more oriented to social service, or reducing the number of citizen complaints and improving community relations, are contradictory to the self-image and style of male policing. Thus it appears that males are adjusting to the change either by denying the females as officers or, as the minority are doing, by accepting women into the group as long as they blend into the "image."

One other question attempted to ascertain whether males (and females) regard the women as equally capable of policing effectively.. Informants were asked whether risk should be a factor in the placement of females. Prior to this question, officers had been asked to list the various job assignments in the department according to degree of risk. The Uniform Patrol Division (evening and morning watches) were almost universally considered the most dangerous. The Fugitive and SWAT teams were also ranked high for potential risk. Most men initially responded that females should be placed anywhere, "since if they're police officers they should go in all positions" (white male, Detective, age 33). "If you're going to pay the same, they should have the same risks" (white male, Detective, age 28). However, in almost all interviews, comments such as these were followed by statements that "if I was personally in charge" females would not be on the street and would best be employed in in-house positions er on the Juvenile and Sex Crimes squads.

Over one-half of the females stated that they should be assigned irregardless of risk although several women included in their responses the idea that placement in general should be more individually oriented, that everyone in the bureau should be assigned on the basis of his or her abilities and personality. Many add that further training in the martial arts should be included at the police academy. Most of the women who do not believe risk should be considered use the same economic rationale as the males:

> Should be anywhere if paid the same salary. Women should go anywhere the brass decides to put them. (white female, Uniform, age 24)

Females who feel that risk should be a factor

The Risk Factor

Should Risk be a Factor in the Placement of Females?

	Yes		No	
	No.	%	No.	%
Females	6	46	7	54
Males[a]	25	68	26	70[b]

Table 18

[a] Male responses exceed 100 percent because they were often a combination of "yes" and "no," e.g., "Yes, it would be a factor if I was running it, but no, if equal pay should have equal risk."

[b] Ten percent did not qualify their negative response; 60 percent stated that risk should not be a factor since females receive equal pay.

concurrently believe that female officers do belong on the street although certain areas of the city, such as the larger government housing projects, would best be patrolled by males.

From the information given above concerning females' self-image and their preference for male partners, it may appear surprising that less than half expressed a desire to be assigned to lower risk positions. This apparent inconsistency may be resolved by also acknowledging the female officers' awareness of males' disapproval of them on the street. Even if the women agree, it is doubtful that they would verbalize it since they are constantly placed in a defensive posture by the males. Furthermore, it should be noted again that almost all females stressed that job placement in the bureau should be more attuned to each individual's aptitude and character, a comment not made by male informants.

How do police officers feel that the public views female police? Most male officers, as the following indicates, are overwhelmingly convinced that the public regards the uniformed females as a joke and as incapable of performing police duties:

> When a policewoman passes, they laugh and make jokes like, "I'd like to see her arrest me." (white, Detective, age 36)

> People consider it a joke. They come up and tell me there's no way that a woman can handle the situation. (white, Detective, age 31)

> People have come up and asked me, "How can they let her be a police officer? How can she handle herself?" (white, Uniform, age 28)

> Most of the public react to her more as a WOMAN than as a police officer. They don't raise their voices or fly off the

handle. Most don't consider them as
competent and for instance would prefer a male if someone's breaking into
their house. (white, Uniform, age 23)

A few male officers took the opposing stance and
emphasized the positive reaction of the public toward female police:

I think they like them. I've seen a
lot of calls where they relate to females better. The man doesn't feel a
threat; therefore she can deal with
the person and the problem instead of
getting into a macho thing. (white,
Uniform, age 27)

Female public see it as a step toward
equal rights. They seem to like it.
Male public are just optimists, waiting
to see what's going to happen. Other
men are scared because in situations
of confrontation, they're afraid she
will use her gun. (black, Uniform, age
27)

No female informant expressed a belief that
the public is entirely positive in its acceptance
of females in policing. In fact, several women
believe that they are being judged entirely negatively:

They view us as a freak. Something odd.
Something to say, "how cute." They don't
respect the authority of females.
(white, Uniform, age 24)

Kind of as a joke; the men laugh, a lot
of the women are envious but a lot of
women who really know themselves, hate
to see women working on a beat because
you lose your identity as a woman when
you're out there. (white, plainclothes,
age 28)

However, most responses are not entirely negative

and indicate a mixed reaction from the public:

> I think that they're finding out that
> women can do the job but there are
> some calls where they say, "I was ex-
> pecting a policeman." Most have a good
> attitude but some view women with more
> fear (pistol). (white, Uniform, age 28)

> Probably as a joke. Driving along, they
> laugh and make comments. But on the job,
> a lot of people look at us as both police
> officers and women. They stop cussing.
> Some have said they'd rather have a man.
> On the whole, the public has reacted
> pretty positively. Some call out, "Honey
> what are you doing out there?" (white,
> Uniform, age 26)

> There are some who look at you like what
> kind of police are you? But I'd say 90
> percent end up seeing me as a police
> officer after I've talked to them and
> they get confidence in me. (white,
> Uniform, age 27)

> The women public think female police can
> understand better but the males think of
> it as a big joke. When I'm riding with
> another female, they go along with you:
> with a male partner, you have more trou-
> ble. They don't want anything to do with
> you. They just see you as not there,
> that there's only one police officer.
> (black, Uniform, age 29)

Lastly, the officers were asked whether they
feel that the introduction of females has affected
the public's general view of the police. The
question was posed since one of the advocating
arguments for having women in policing is the view
that their presence, by softening the image of the
police, might help bridge the gap between the
police and the public. Responses might also dis-
close major changes in the police subculture which
would affect police-community relations. The data

presented in Table 19 indicate that most officers do not believe that female officers have significantly altered the relationship between the police and the public. The explanations given by males for their opinion concerning lack of change often contradicted their previous assertion that the public does not regard females as bona fide police. These officers concurrently believe that to the public, police are police, and therefore the introduction of females would not necessitate any revision of opinion of police in general. "When in uniform they don't really care if it's a man or a woman" (white male, Uniform, age 25). Other males feel that no change had resulted since females are not regarded as true police by the public. The few males who responded "yes" either verbalized a view that women have softened the image held by the public or have lowered the esteem in which the department had previously been held.

The women who answered negatively did not generally elaborate beyond saying that the public considers females within the same image. Females who felt that a change in opinion has occurred express the view that females are assisting in combating alienation:

> I think the public is a little more
> interested in the police and there's
> the curiosity and community relations
> type atmosphere with people asking
> what women are doing. (white, plain-
> clothes, age 24)

> I think it's given the public a bit
> of a softer image since women won't use
> physical strength as much. (white, Uni-
> form, age 28)

However, the general consensus from both sexes was that the public does not have an entirely positive view of females in policing and that the females have not significantly altered the public's view of police officers in general. The officers' opinions above do contradict data from other studies (Breece and Garrett 1974; Bloch and

Women Police and the Public

Have Female Police Affected the
Public's View of Police _in toto_?

	Yes		No	
	No.	%	No.	%
Females	5	38	8	62
Males	6	16	31	84
Total sample	11	22	39	78

Table 19

Anderson 1974) who found that the implementation of females into patrol operations resulted in an improved public image. This may in fact be true in Atlanta. However, it is important to note that the officers do not believe so. Alienation, from the police view, has not decreased: thus one possible effect of introducing females into police work is minimized.

The comments by officers concerning the public's presumed perception of females included several interesting concepts which will be elaborated upon in the next chapter. The hesitancy of male officers (and allegedly, the public) to accept females in positions of authority appears to grow out of cultural mores and institutions which preclude a total acceptance of women as uniformed police, a role that symbolizes and embodies force and authority in our society.

SUMMARY AND CONCLUSIONS

Previous studies of all-male police departments have tended to stress the masculine role of
police officers in this country. Aggressiveness
and physical strength have been perceived as a
part of the police image. Prior research has
also emphasized the group solidarity of police
officers, a cohesiveness based upon camaraderie
between members of an all-male group. The present
study was therefore interested in whether this
police in-group strength has been exaggerated and
in what effects, if any, female officers have had
upon solidarity and alienation.

It is the conclusion of this study that the
incorporation of women officers has effected little
change in either the cohesiveness of the group or
in its sense of isolation from the public. However, the phenomenon of women in law enforcement is
so recent that conclusions must be regarded as
based upon only preliminary data requiring a follow-up study in several years. At this early
stage, it is this researcher's contention that
police solidarity has not been affected by the
introduction of women. The latter have been accul-
turated into the group's attitudes and behavior,
but remain in a subordinate position in the males'
eyes. The result has been the formation of a
sexually stratified group.

Thus the women's lack of impact in policing
appears to be the result of two somewhat contra-
dicting factors. The women have not affected the
males' self-image or police-public relations because they have not been accepted as true police
officers. Simultaneously, they have been accul-
turated into the group's behavioral and attitudinal patterns. Therefore, in a sense, they are
accepted as members of a closed group--insiders
who have seen the real world. However, because
they are not regarded as equals, the police group

maintains its social isolation by adapting to these "outsiders" through acculturation and sexual stratification. Almost every female and male in the sample believed that alienation still exists between the police and the public. Few officers feel that women have affected citizens' attitudes toward the Atlanta Bureau of Police Services, and almost all officers express negative feelings toward the public thus reaffirming the view that the police, as a group, remain alienated from the public.

Many factors contribute to solidarity within a group that is divided both racially and sexually. The following summary of policing in Atlanta should elucidate many of these forces that promote in-group rigidity and should also indicate how female officers, through their acculturation, have become more cynical, more conservative, and more alienated from the public.

Atlanta offered a unique background for a description of policing. Given the breakdown within the structural organization and the white officers' almost total disloyalty to the top administrators, one might expect to have found a lessening of police solidarity. However, the opposite seems to have occurred. The dissension within the department and the covert racial fissioning have been alluded to throughout the study. The fact remains that although few white officers feel a loyalty to the macrostructure of the bureau or ties of camaraderie with many black officers, their identity as police officers remains intact. Although some white officers stated that they no longer view policing as a role which they never cast off, no informant throughout the year ever expressed the feeling that his or her self-identity as a police officer has decreased nor, as a result, that they feel less alienated from non-police.

Interestingly, disloyalty to the structure of the department has probably increased the solidarity among officers and the alienation from, and

hostility toward, the public. Shared feelings of
total dissatisfaction with the internal political
situation are verbalized in almost every conversation between white officers, thus providing a
further common link. The white Atlanta officers
believe that the white public is either apathetic
toward or ignorant of the policies instituted by
the commissioner. The black public is generally
assumed to admire and advocate the commissioner's
programs. This further alienates the officers from
a citizenry which they feel does not care about
their plight. Other studies (Banton 1964; Skolnick
1967; Rubinstein 1973; Wambaugh 1970, 1972) have
mentioned the dissatisfaction that police officers
feel toward their jobs and the public. Thus, a
certain amount of griping appears to be normal
among police. However, the degree of discontent
among the white officers in Atlanta appears to be
more intense, a conclusion based upon their own
articulation of an increased sense of malaise
directly caused by the current administration.

The marked degree of demoralization was also
apparent in the account of the watches in Chapters
4 and 5, showing that only a small percentage of the
shift is actually spent on policing duties. White
uniformed officers are doing the minimal amount of
patrol work possible although their calls usually
only involve one to three hours of the shift. The
detectives rarely encounter a case which requires
anything beyond the most perfunctory investigation.
It is not uncommon for a detective watch to pass
without one radio request for the services of that
squad. Therefore, for both uniformed officers and
detectives, a large proportion of their shift is
available for either patrolling or personal activities.

The Atlanta officers observed usually chose
non-policing pursuits and participated in many nonregulation actions. These are so common and widespread that they have become normalized within the
group. Although few black officers were observed,
they too indulged in many of these practices.
Thus it seems that personal activities constitute

an important part of the police officers' occupation. It is probable that in other departments, where morale is higher, these non-policing undertakings are not quite as frequent. The sharing of these activities undoubtedly contributes to the solidarity of the group; it also reinforces the boundary between police and the public who are presumed to be ignorant of the extent of "personal" time consuming "city" time.

Policing, because it upholds the status quo with legitimate authority, also alienates the police from the public. Previous studies (Cumming, Cumming and Edell 1969; Patrick 1972; Skolnick 1967) have concentrated upon the isolating effects of authority. The enforcer of laws in a democratic society where the emphasis is on individual freedom will always be regarded with a degree of distrust. Given the atmosphere in the United States today, with the recent liberalization of the judicial criminal system and a reemphasis upon civil liberties, both the male and female officers in Atlanta view themselves almost as pariahs in society, merely because they perform their occupational duties. Officers state that they frequently do not tell neighbors or potential romantic partners that they are police officers. Further study of the public's attitudes toward police would reveal whether there has been increased hostility to law enforcement agents as a result of the legal and ideological changes of the very recent past. A study of any group in contemporary society must not disregard the feedback to and from other groups and social institutions. If, in fact,the public's alienation from the police has increased in the last fifteen years, it may be due to changes that have occurred within the political, legal, and social institutions of the wider society.

If cognizant of the isolating effects of authority, the Atlanta officers ignore it and frequently flaunt their power. When an officer speeds through the city streets, flagrantly disobeying all traffic rules, without cause, he often says that it is all right for him since he is the law. "After all, who's going to give me a citation?"

The nature of the job also provides a unique
view of mankind; almost constantly officers are
faced with people's transgressions. As one of
Wambaugh's fictional officers concludes:

> You can't exaggerate the closeness of
> our dealings with people. We see them
> when nobody else sees them, when they're
> being born and dying and fornicating and
> drunk . . . we see people when they're
> taking anything of value from other people
> and when they're without shame or very
> much ashamed . . . well then you really
> know. Of course you get clannish and
> associate with others who know. It's
> only natural. (1970: 171)

A constant exposure to the negative aspects of man
certainly has affected the Atlanta officers' general attitudes toward people and life. When a
police officer sees a man walking down the street
in Atlanta (s)he sees either a potential victim or,
more commonly, an individual who has or will commit
a crime. Suspicion and cynicism abound in almost
every conversation between officers, both male and
female. As indicated by most of the officers'
comments, they are well aware of the effect that
their occupational environment has had upon their
attitudes toward the public and life. Their responses have indicated a high frequency of conservatism, cynicism, and alienation. Most informants
claimed that these feelings have been generated
through policing and were nonexistent prior to
membership in the department. The officers' anti-
pathetic and apathetic feelings about the public
do become apparent in their interactions with the
citizenry which undoubtedly increases the emnity--
a vicious circle which shows no sign of abating.

When an officer answers a call, (s)he carries
a gun and the legal right to use it. There must
be an element of fear in most citizens when
interacting with an individual who carries a
deadly weapon. Officers answering calls do not

appear as individuals; their uniforms, weapons, badges, and impersonal manner all act to proclaim them as members of a group. No uniformed officer, and only a few of the detectives observed, ever identified themselves by name to the citizens on a case. Several officers commented on the anonymity of their roles after handling calls. They stated that the public does not view them as people but only as police officers.

The depersonalization of the profession has been increased by the age of specialization and the disappearance, in Atlanta, of the cop who walked a regular beat, knew everybody by name, and was known by everyone. The social amenities at encounters between the police and the public today are few. Personalization has given way to professionalism. Hahn (1974: 24) notes that as police departments become more professionalized, they also become more self-contained and less reliant upon the assistance of the public. The growing specialization of police functions reduces the importance of information obtained from, and contacts with, civilians.

In Atlanta, the officer, male or female, duly takes a report, and usually appears to be emotionally aloof from the victim's plight. The number of reports written produces a tediousness and a boredom with most cases. Most calls are regarded as spurious with doubt focused upon either the victim's veracity or the legal solidity of a case, which, according to the police, must withstand a veritable onslaught from a leftist judicial system. Furthermore, the role of police officer is not that of social worker or psychologist. It does not readily accommodate emotional involvement. The victim sees only a uniformed person taking a report without much interest; the officer sees yet another citizen who (s)he feels is only using him and will shortly return to the normal apathy or hostility. "The same ones that call you pig, want you when their car's stolen." Scaglion (1973) in his survey of police-community relations found that citizens who gave police a bad rating often did complain about the officer's unconcerned attitude. When the officer regarded a call as merely routine and the complainant considered it to be important, the latter was unhappy with the police officer. Most of the white Atlanta officers seldom appear to regard a call as important, particularly on the frequent domestic disturbance cases which the participants undoubtedly view as such. Thus public dissatisfaction probably increases, and the gap between the police and the citizenry is reinforced.

The legal and the departmental changes that have reduced police power were enumerated in Chapter 3. Presumably one of the expected outcomes of these restrictions upon police authority was to help bridge the gap between the police and the public, with a greater emphasis upon public relations as the incidence of brutality and harassment declined. Few incidents of brutality were observed during the field work, as compared to the policing style of the past as depicted by the mass media and recounted by veteran officers. However, the expected outcome of improved relations with the public has not occurred in Atlanta. Actually the degree of alienation may have increased since officers today must repress their prejudices and hostilities except among themselves. There is an increased frustration with policing which further isolates the occupational group; officers believe that the efficacy of their role has been thwarted and that they are functioning merely as puppets for a radicalized judicial system and a racist police administration.

Today, the officers are expected to be civil at all calls and must largely restrain from any temptation to employ force. Their frustrations are ameliorated at the frequent meetings between officers--which act almost as rites of solidification--for the expression of mutual sympathy and mutual berating of the system and the citizens. The insider-outsider gap increases as the officers experience feelings of abandonment in the present climate of civil liberties and civil rights.

The environmental experiences of policing in Atlanta were elaborated upon in Chapters 4-6. It has been shown that most calls involve members of several subcultures with life-styles far different from that in which most officers were raised and presently live. Further study of a police department in a small town or an affluent suburb might reveal a lesser degree of alienation between the police and the public. In the city of Atlanta, however, a high percentage of encounters between police and citizens involve lower-class blacks and members of the wino-tramp subculture. Repeated exposure to squalor and overt disorganization has promoted or intensified prejudices. "Can you imagine calling the police for something like that?" "Did you see all those kids awake so late at night?" "How can anyone live with so much filth?" The comments directed at those segments of the public with whom the officers spend most policing time often extend to rather shocking statements that equate certain groups with animals and their homes with zoos. It was not unusual for an officer to express a belief that walls should be constructed around the housing projects and the inhabitants left entirely alone to annihilate themselves with their seemingly violent style of interaction. Niederhoffer (1969: 223) believes that police officers do accept a minority group's way of life on its own terms to the extent of not formally reporting many violent incidents in black and Puerto Rican areas because the officers recognize that violence has become the accepted way of life in these communities and victims will not prosecute. Atlanta officers do indeed recognize this fact but certainly not in the cultural relativistic framework that Niederhoffer proposes.

The winos do not appear to be regarded with hatred so much as contempt. They are also seen as less than human. In the late 1960's the hippies, another target for ill-feeling and violence, labeled "maggots," were also characterized as animals. As Chapter 7 indicated, other groups of society, the mainstream, are not viewed affectionately either. Officers seldom ascribe negative labels to those middle- and upper-class persons encountered, but the latter are regarded as unsympathetic and unappreciative of the role that police must play.

Therefore, the nature of the role that police have as enforcer, authority figure, impersonal representative of the law; the actions that provoke the need for an officer's presence; the frustration of white officers in response to recent judicial and departmental changes which have hampered their previous style of policing; and the alien nature of the subcultures most frequently encountered--all contribute to the isolation of the white police officers as a group and to the socialization of women police into police attitudes and behavior. Almost all members feel alienated from the public, and it has been shown that male-female officer homogeneity in other attitudes also occurs. Several of these shared opinions were indicated earlier including an almost universal expression of alienation manifested in officers' responses to questions concerning the police and the public. The widely held self-image of conservatism which many officers believe to have resulted from policing was further evident in the marked uniformity of statements concerning capital punishment and the judicial and penal systems. The isolating effects of the occupation may be further evidenced by the extremely high divorce rate found in the sample and the recent incidence of in-group marriages.

The white officers in Atlanta, male and female, continue to exist as a strongly isolated group. Despite embitterment and estrangement from the department as a structure and the introduction of female officers, the solidarity of the group survives due to the many aspects of the occupation outlined above. The result is a police department which has both stratified sexually and fissioned racially to a great extent but remains alienated from the public.

Women in Policing

In Chapter 8, the responses of the male officers interviewed in the sample revealed their non-acceptance of women as police. Observations throughout the year reinforce the quantitative results. The male officer does not see an effective fellow officer in a uniformed female. The following incident, which was repeated in various forms throughout the research, exemplifies this attitude. When a detective is going on a pull (arrest) he may call for a Uniform car to meet him at the arrest location for backup. On one occasion, a homicide detective expressed disappointment and contempt when the backup unit arrived and a diminutive female approached him for instructions. "I call for a backup and this is what I get." He did not feel secure or assisted by what he perceived as inadequate physical strength, or the appearance of it.

This lack of confidence in females is acted out daily. Many officers rapidly converge upon hearing a female receive a call and frequently end up largely taking over. In the sexually mixed detective units that were observed, the females assumed a subservient behavior style when partnered with males. The male always drove, dominated calls, and dictated the watch's activities. The female officer almost always handled the paper work, in some instances merely recording the responses to questions posed by the male partner. The females' role is superceded by the male officers. The male view may be summarized by their oft-repeated expression, "You're not really a po' lice until you get your butt beat . . . and beat one in return." This remark was often followed by, "And the women in this department make sure that they don't ever get into a good fight."

The result of this male lack of acceptance of females as equals is that the men frequently assume a sexually bantering style when interacting with female officers. Unlike the racial exclusion at 59's and dinner breaks, one does frequently observe female officers as part of the group.

196

However, there is a noticeable difference in the style and content of conversation that are male-male and those that are male-female. In the latter, the male officers frequently make sexual innuendos or assume a teasing attitude that might be equated with an older brother. It readily becomes obvious that females are simply not regarded as one of the fellows, at work or socially.

It is difficult to ascertain whether the presence of women has affected male officers' style of policing. With the many legal, administrative, and racial changes that have taken place recently, it is impossible to isolate one factor as the direct cause of the white males' behavioral and attitudinal modifications. The white males are, at the present time, in a disillusioned state of mind, shown in the frequent rule infractions and verbalizations of discontent. Female officers are undoubtedly one source of dissatisfaction. However, the men do not appear to have been as affected by the existence of female officers as they are deeply upset by the limitations upon police power and the increase in black officers. The men have coped psychologically with the presence of women in all facets of police work by dealing with them as subordinates. The men in the sample feel overwhelmingly that their self-image as officers has not been affected by female officers because the latter are not regarded by the males as bona fide police.

The men do not modify their behavior when female officers are present. If a uniformed officer has a particularly rough manner of handling prisoners, he maintains that style when a female officer is also on the call. Although incidents involving physical force are extremely rare, the males interviewed believe that legal and administrative decisions, not the presence of female officers, have produced the new, less physical policing style. The log presentation in this study has indicated that few calls responded to by the Atlanta police during the year of observation involved the need for use of physical force. The

197

dramatic type of policing depicted in the mass
media is indeed far from the reality in Atlanta.
Most cases handled by uniformed patrol officers are
accidents, larcenies, false alarms, drunks, and
fight calls. Only the latter offer potential danger, and in Atlanta most disputes observed were
domestic verbal quarrels which only required the
officer to play the role of mediator. The detectives are exposed to some danger and potential
violence when making an arrest. Since these infrequent occasions are well organized with sufficient
manpower available, the danger is actually minimal.
Most detective work is performed after the fact and
thus the need to use physical force is negligible.

The question of whether women have affected
the incidence of brutality must be viewed with an
understanding of the actual rarity of dramatic,
violent incidents that might evoke the use of
physical measures. The vast majority of police
work is paper work. In the occasional instances
when physical strength can be used, male officers
do employ it. Males frequently shove and man-
handle prisoners in order to get them into the
squad cars whereas the females usually employ verbal strategies. It should be noted that although
no female officer who was observed roughed up suspects or prisoners, one female officer was mentioned by several male officers as being both
masculine in appearance and in her physical style
of policing.

If there is indeed less frequent use of physical force today, it is probably due to the legal
changes and to the officers' feelings of abandonment by the administration. The male officer who
brutalizes a suspect no longer has the support of
the courts, his chief, or his immediate superiors.
It is this study's conclusion that any change in
policing style should not be attributed to the
presence of females. The males do not allow the
females to exhibit any unique style since in most
calls which might evoke a more peaceful response
by the female officer, the male dominates the
incident. Thus, the men are rarely exposed to a
less physical style of policing used by most

females.

How do the women respond to their obvious lack
of acceptance as equals? On the whole, the females do not appear offended by the males' backup
or their dominating attitude. Several of the
women working on patrol confided that they did not
want to be there and would much prefer an in-house
or detective assignment. The women appear to
recognize an apparent inadequacy in their job performance as exemplified by their preference for
male partners. However, some optimistic females
did believe that in time they would be wholly
accepted into the ranks and effect some changes,
such as improving police-community relations by
altering the male officers' macho self-image and
style of policing. Others resent the teasing,
belittling attitude and behavior of their male
colleagues. Several women who either resigned from
the department or were contemplating such an action
described this failure to be taken seriously as
their major complaint.

Women do not generally patrol in the same way
as male officers. Many of the reasons for this
may be in the protective attitude and behavior of
their male peers who rarely permit them to police
alone. But several women were observed who deliberately drove slowly to a potentially violent call.
No female observed ever tried to find law breakers,
by driving down dark alleys in the hope of locating
some criminal activity, for example. Some were
overtly doubtful of their ability to function
effectively in uniform. On every violent call
during the year, a male was present at the scene.
In almost every such incident he took over the
call. Women performed the paper work equally pro-
ficiently on accidents, larcenies, burglary, and
robbery reports. However rare their occurrence,
there are fight calls and other incidents in which
physical strength is important, if only as a deterrent. The women observed did not have self-confidence in their physical capabilities. Their lack
of training in the martial arts at the Police
Academy may contribute to feelings of inadequacy.

Due to the protectiveness of the male officers, the females seldom have the opportunity to perform alone which might improve both their self-image and the males' attitude.

The female plainclothes officers and uniformed patrol officers do, in one sense, police in the same manner as the men; their patrolling activity is also frequently abandoned in lieu of personal pursuits. Several of the females observed, both white and black, spent a lengthy percentage of their shifts at home either watching TV or engaged in conversation with female partners. The topics discussed rarely included policing; instead, the women talked about their children, husbands or boyfriends, clothes, and other subjects which male officers regard as "woman talk."

As Chapter 8 indicated, most female informants do not believe that their self-image as police officers is equivalent to their male peers' self-view. The essential difference, many women said, is that to them policing is just a job whereas they believe that most male officers are enmeshed in the macho police-officer role. The women do not appear to try to emulate the males' more physical style. However, their voices do become more gruff and impersonal when interacting with members of the public. Either consciously or unconsciously, many discard the mannerisms that society considers to be feminine.

Policing has had its effects upon the women who have joined the department. Many female informants admit to a growing conservatism which is reflected in their responses to questions concerning the judicial and penal systems, capital punishment, victims and perpetrators of crimes. Almost every woman encountered throughout the year expressed some negative feelings toward non-police. A larger number of the female officers' social contacts are fellow officers. Most single women date male officers, and almost one-half of the married females have husbands who are police officers. Several women felt an inability in either maintaining or forming friendships with

civilians. Some had friends from their pre-
policing days who had terminated the relationship,
expressing amazement and disdain of their occupational choice. Female officers frequently discussed their cynical and distrustful attitude
toward people which they felt had affected their
personal relationships. They ascribed these
feelings to the experiences of policing and felt
that being police officers had changed them in
some ways that alienated them from non-police.

Several women had been divorced since becoming
police officers and expressed the view that their
occupation has caused the marriage to break up.
They attributed it to several factors. The women
complained that they had difficulty relating to
men who were not police officers and did not share
their view of people and life. Secondly, the
ratio of males to females in the bureau is very
high. The men's flirtatious manner can be grati-
fying to a woman, and, particularly in the confines
of a police car, a threat to any marriage.

Thus the effects of policing upon the female
officers can reach into all aspects of their lives.
Although most females claim to regard policing as
just an eight-hour-a-day job, the attitude changes
that occur during working hours are not discarded
after work. Despite their inability to be assimi-
lated into the group by the males and despite
their own recognition of inadequacies in their job
performance, the acculturation of the women into
the policing world has caused modifications in
their attitudes, behavior, and social relationships.

A part of the women's inability to police
effectively stems from the public's view of females in uniform. Although this research did not
include interviews with civilians, my observation
indicated that the members of the public with whom
the police have the most contact appeared to
regard the female officers as a curiosity, a joke,
and as unable to handle physical situations
effectively. As several informants stated in

Chapter 8, the public seems to see a woman, not a police officer, and inevitably turns first to a male officer if one is present. Several female officers complained that they are virtually ignored at some calls by both the male officers and by the citizens. It is true that no perpetrator was heard to utter, "No lady police is going to arrest me," but in felonious arrest cases a male officer was always at the scene. The only observed arrests physically made by females were drunks.

The females, as stated earlier, have adopted many of the attitudes toward the public and toward law enforcement issues that characterize male police. Observation destroyed earlier contentions that women are helping to bridge the gap between the police and the citizenry. The public appeared to accept the authority of females only within certain limits. Fortunately, a male officer was always present when the female's power seemed in jeopardy. The females do manifest a similar behavior style and attitude toward the public as the males, although they depend more upon their mental agility as opposed to brute force. But any difference in policing style is minimized by the frequent presence of male officers at females' calls and the rarity of encounters in which physical force is a factor. Females were not more sympathetic to victims, even victims of rape, as might be expected. In fact, at times the women appeared to be less affected than the men. The females have experienced the same negative stimuli as the males and have developed similar hardened attitudes toward people and their impoverished lives. Therefore, on the one side, the public does not seem to regard female officers as bona fide police; on the other, female officers perpetuate the existing police-public relationship by developing the same attitudes and behavior styles toward the citizenry that are exhibited by their male colleagues.

Women in Policing--The Future

Before suggesting some practical measures

which could be taken by urban police departments to improve the efficacy of females in policing, the reasons behind the failure of women to achieve an equal status with males as police officers must be examined. Since the problems may be rooted in the wider sociocultural values and norms, the effectiveness of any of the policies outlined below will be limited.

In the last fifty years there have been many changes in society's conception of the role of women. In many fields, women have achieved an equality with their male peers. Females in many social, legal, political, and religious institutions hold positions of authority. Thus, it is not the authority element of the officer's role per se which precludes acceptance of women in policing at this time. However, the image of police authority as it has developed in North America was closely identified with physical macho power. Cross-cultural research could be employed to examine the reception of female officers in other countries, such as Great Britain where physical force is not the primary image of police authority. In these countries, and in small towns in America where the local constabulary are involved in social relations with many of the citizenry, one might expect to find a more ready acceptance of females in the policing role.

In Atlanta and other cities in the United States, however, the masculine element of policing has dominated the image of police officers. Females simply do not present this image in American society. Given a tall and hefty woman and a short, slightly built man, it is still the male who connotes strength and manliness simply because he is a man. Male officers enculturated with society's image of the female sex and their image of policing find it extremely difficult to reconcile the two and learn to rely upon females as equal partners. Hence, the men are overprotective and limit the role that the women may play.

Thus, the idea or fact of physical inadequacy

is a major impediment to the acceptance of females
into the uniformed policing role and image in the
Atlanta Police Department. Either the view of
females as weaker or the view and self-image of
American police as symbols of physical power will
have to change. If the number of females in
policing grows to equal or exceed the number of
men, the public's general image of police may
change. Or American perception of the female sex
may undergo further revisions--the many concrete
advances that women have made are relatively
recent. The gap between institutional equality and
the ideological perceptual level of the culture may
close in time, producing an image of females that
would be compatible with the role of police officers.

Until that time, women in one-man patrol cars
appear to be a waste of efficiency and money. The
males' overprotectiveness and the public's reaction
limit the females' effectiveness. It is also a
potentially volatile situation which may result in
needless injuries or death. Women are regarded as
acceptable for some detective positions where the
image of strength is not construed by the officers
as being as important. Unfortunately, there is a
basic inequity involved in assigning females
directly to detective squads. Although paid the
same as uniformed officers, the plainclothes officers' positions hold more status within the bureau.

Other possibilities include "team policing"
in which several female officers could do the
followup investigative work operating out of the
zone, in uniform, at uniform pay. Thus, a male
beat officer would handle the initial report and
the sergeant would assign it to a female officer
instead of directing it to a particular detective
squad. This plan would accommodate affirmative
action's required number of females in uniform.
If a female objected to the investigation assignment, she could submit a transfer request to a
patrol car. Since almost every female police
officer encountered during the field work expressed a preference for in-house or PCO positions,
unless the situation for females on uniform patrol

changes dramatically, it is unlikely that this would occur. Another alternative would be two-man police cars with female officers partnered with males. However, it would be advisable to shift the personnel regularly in order to attempt to avoid emotional complications between partners.

If women continue to be assigned to street policing in urban areas, I do have one strong recommendation. The academy period should be extended with prolonged training in the martial arts for female recruits. These classes should continue after graduation with voluntary attendance by female officers. Since many women expressed a desire for additional instruction to improve their ability in physical combat, a large percentage of the female officers would probably attend. The program should also be well publicized in order to inform the citizenry that although female police officers may not appear to be physically strong they are indeed well equipped to handle physical confrontations. The classes would give the women some much needed self-confidence which might be translated into their policing activities. Most importantly, their male peers might accept the women as being more capable of street policing. A comparative study with another urban police department which has an intensive martial arts program for female officers might indicate whether increased physical capability promotes a greater acceptance of females as police officers.

GLOSSARY

Choir practice: outdoor drinking parties after work.

Crack: as a noun; a place to sleep, relax, or pursue personal activities during "working" hours.

Day watch: daytime work shift. Detectives, 8 a.m. - 4 p.m.; Uniformed, 7 a.m. - 3 p.m.

Evening watch: evening work shift. Detectives, 4 p.m. - 12 a.m.; Uniformed, 3 p.m. - 11 p.m.

Full of dead air: refers to no calls on police radio.

Hmmy: officers' designation for case they believe lacks credibility or involves no avenues for investigation.

Hot load: putting extra gun powder into bullets (against police regulations).

Jamming the radio: keying the microphone. Used to show hostility toward certain officers.

Morning watch: late night work shift. Detectives, 12 a.m. - 8 a.m.; Uniformed, 11 p.m. - 7 a.m.

Off days: days off.

PCO: plainclothes officer.

Pimp: to inform, snitch.

Pull: an arrest.

<u>Reggie</u>: white officers' designation for Commissioner Eaves.

<u>Roustabout</u>: uniformed officer without an assigned beat car.

<u>Shop</u> (<u>the</u>): gasoline station and auto repair center for police vehicles.

<u>Trim</u>: females considered to be sexually available for male police officers.

<u>Umbrella car</u>: uniformed officer(s)' car whose "beat" includes one half of a zone.

<u>War stories</u>: tales about past police exploits.

<u>Watch change</u>: shift change.

<u>Zone</u>: precinct.

APPENDIX 2

FREQUENTLY USED RADIO SIGNALS

"24": demented person.

"28": drunk.

"29": fight.

"30": DUI-driving under influence.

"39": information for officer.

"41": vehicle accident.

"44": robbery.

"45": larceny.

"48": dead person.

"49": rape.

"50": shooting.

"51": stabbing.

"63": officer in trouble-help call.

BIBLIOGRAPHY

Albrecht, Stan, Howard Bahr and Bruce Chadwick
    1977   "Public Stereotyping of Sex Roles,
                Personality Characteristics, and
                Occupations," Sociology and Social
                Research, 61, 2.

Alex, Nicholas
    1969   Black in Blue: A Study of the Negro
                Policeman, New York: Appleton-Century-
                Crofts.

Banton, Michael
    1964   The Policeman in the Community, London:
                Tavistock Publications.

Beizel, Herbert
    1974   "The Investigation and Prosecution of
                Police Corruption," Journal of Crimi-
                nal Law and Criminology, 65(2): 135-
                156.

Bittner, Egon
    1967   "The Police on Skid-Row: A Study of
                Peace Keeping," American Sociological
                Review, 32: 699-715.

    1974   "Esprits de Corps and the Code of
                Secrecy," The Police Community, eds.
                Jack and Sharon Goldsmith. Palisades:
                Pacific Palisades Publisher.

Bloch, Peter and Deborah Anderson
    1974   Policewoman on Patrol: Final Report,
                Washington, D.C.: Police Foundation.

Blumberg, Abraham
    1969   "The Criminal Court as Organization
                and Communication System," Crime and
                Justice in Society, ed. Richard
                Quinney. Boston: Little, Brown and
                Company.

Breece, Constance and Gerald R. Garrett
1974   "Women in Policing: Changing Per-
         spectives on the Role," Unpublished
         manuscript.

Burnham, D.
1972   "More Women Joining the Police Force
         in U.S.," New York Times, June 6.

Carlson, Helena and Robert Thayer, A.C. Germann
1971   "Social Attitudes and Personality
         Differences among Members of Two
         Kinds of Police Departments (Innova-
         tive vs. Traditional) and Students,"
         The Journal of Criminal Law, Crimi-
         nology and Police Science. 62(4):
         564-567.

Chambers, M.
1973   "On a Mixed Police Patrol in Midtown,"
         New York Times, November 21.

Chevigny, Paul
1969   Police Power, New York: Vintage Books.

Clark, John P.
1969   "Isolation of the Police: A Comparison
         of the British and American Situations,"
         Crime and Justice in Society, ed.
         Richard Quinney. Boston: Little,
         Brown and Company.

Cumming, Elaine and Ian Cumming, Laura Edell
1969   "Policeman as Philosopher, Guide and
         Friend," Crime and Justice in Society,
         ed. Richard Quinney. Boston: Little,
         Brown and Company.

Fagerstrom, D.
1969   "Policewomen's Viewpoint of Behavioral
         Problems," Law and Order, 17: 88-95.

1970   "Wider Horizons for Policewomen,"
         Law and Order, 18: 81-83.

Goldsmith, Jack and Sharon
    1974   The Police Community, Palisades:
            Pacific Palisades Publishers.

Goldstein, Joseph
    1960   "Police Discretion Not to Invoke the
            Criminal Process: Low Visibility
            Decisions in the Administration of
            Justice," The Yale Law Journal, 69:
            574-75.

Greenwald, Judith and Harriet Connolly
    1974   "Policewomen on Patrol: New York City,"
            Unpublished manuscript.

Hahn, Harlan
    1974   "A Profile of Urban Police," The
            Police Community, eds. Jack and
            Sharon Goldsmith. Palisades: Pacific
            Palisades Publishers.

Horne, Peter
    1975   Women in Law Enforcement, Springfield:
            Charles C. Thomas.

Jenkins, Herbert T.
    1973   Forty Years on the Force: 1932-1972,
            Atlanta: National Graphics Inc.

LaFave, Wayne R.
    1969   "Police Discretion," Crime and Jus-
            tice in Society, ed. Richard Quinney.
            Boston: Little, Brown and Company.

Levine, James F.
    1971   "Implementing Legal Policies Through
            Operant Conditioning: The Case of
            Police Practices," Law and Society
            Review, 6(2): 195-221.

Mathias and Anderson
    1973   From Horse to Helicopter, Atlanta:
            Georgia State University Press.

Milton, Caroline
   1972   Women in Policing, Washington, DC.:
             Police Foundation.

   1974   Women in Policing: A Manual,
             Washington, D.C.: Police Foundation.

Niederhoffer, Arthur
   1967   Behind the Shield, New York: Doubleday.

   1969   "On the Job," Crime and Justice in
             Society, ed. Richard Quinney. Boston:
             Little, Brown and Company.

_____ and A. Blumberg, eds.

   1973   The Ambivalent Force: Perspectives on
             the Police, San Francisco: Rinehart
             Press.

Owings, Chloe
   1969   Women Police, New Jersey: Patterson
             Smith.

Patrick, Clarence
   1972   "The Police in Modern Society," The
             Police, Crime and Society, ed.
             Clarence Patrick. Springfield,
             Illinois: Charles C. Thomas.

Piliavin, Irving and Scott Briar
   1969   "Police Encounters with Juveniles,"
             Crime and Justice in Society, ed.
             Richard Quinney. Boston: Little,
             Brown and Company.

Quinney, Richard
   1969   Crime and Justice in Society, Boston:
             Little, Brown and Company.

Radano, Gent
   1968   Walking the Beat, New York: World
             Publishing Company.

Rankin, Robert S.
    1972   "Social Control," The Police, Crime
            and Society, ed. Clarence Patrick.
            Springfield, Illinois: Charles C.
            Thomas.

Rink, S.E.
    1963   "Arresting Females: The Policewoman's
            Story," Law and Order, 1: 6-7.

Roucek, Joseph S. and Clarence Patrick
    1972   "The Police Officer and the United
            States Constitution," The Police,
            Crime and Society, ed. Clarence
            Patrick. Springfield, Illinois:
            Charles C. Thomas.

Rubinstein, Jonathon
    1973   City Police, New York: Ballantine
            Books.

Scaglion, Richard
    1973   "Data Report to the Police-Community
            Relations Project," Pittsburgh, Pa.,
            Duplicated.

Sherman, Lewis T.
    1975   "An Evaluation of Policewomen on
            Patrol in a Suburban Police Depart-
            ment," Journal of Police Science and
            Administration, 3(4): 434-438.

Sichel, Joyce and Lucy Friedman, Janet Quint,
Michael Smith
    1977   "Women on Patrol: A Pilot Study of
            Policing Performances in New York
            City," Unpublished manuscript.

Skolnick, Jerome H.
    1967   Justice Without Trial: Law Enforce-
            ment in Democratic Society, New York:
            John Wiley and Sons, Inc.

Snow, M.
    1956   "Women's Role in Crime Control," The
            Police Yearbook, 71-79.

Tenny, E.
1953 "Women's Work in Law Enforcement,"
   <u>Journal of Criminal Law, Criminology</u>
   <u>and Police Science</u>, 44: 239-246.

Trojanowicz, Robert C.
1971 "The Policeman's Occupational Personality," <u>Journal of Criminal Law,</u>
   <u>Criminology and Police Science</u>, 62(4):
   551-559.

Trujillo, R.
1973 "Policewomen . . . No Longer Just
   Meter Maids," <u>Criminal Justice News</u>,
   October.

Wambaugh, Joseph
1970 <u>The New Centurions</u>, Boston: Little,
   Brown and Company.

1972 <u>The Blue Knight</u>, Boston: Little, Brown
   and Company.

1973 <u>The Onion Field</u>, New York: Delacorte
   Press.

1975 <u>The Choirboys</u>, New York: Delacorte
   Press.

Washington, Brenda
1974 <u>Deployment of Female Police Officers</u>
   <u>in the United States</u>, Washington,
   D.C.: Police Foundation.

Westley, William A.
1969 "Violence and the Police," <u>Crime and</u>
   <u>Justice in Society</u>, ed. Richard
   Quinney. Boston: Little, Brown and
   Company.

1970 <u>Violence and the Police</u>, Cambridge:
   MIT Press.

Weston, Paul B. and Kenneth M. Wells
1971 <u>Criminal Evidence for Police</u>, New

Jersey: Prentice Hall Inc.

Wilson, James Q.
 1970   "The Police and their Problems: A
          Theory," The Politics of Legal Jus-
          tice, eds. James R. Klonoski, Robert
          I. Mendelsohn. Boston: Little,
          Brown and Company.

 1972   "The Patrolman," Crime and Justice in
          Society, ed. Richard Quinney. Boston:
          Little, Brown and Company.

Wyles, Lilian
 1952   Women at Scotland Yard, London:
          Faber and Faber.

ABOUT THE AUTHOR

Patricia Lynn Weiser Remmington received her Ph.D. in Anthropology from the University of Pittsburgh, 1978. She is an Assistant Professor in the Department of Ethnic Studies at Bowling Green State University, Bowling Green, Ohio where she also teaches courses for the Sociology Department and Women's Studies Program. Married and the mother of two small sons, Dr. Remmington nostalgically recalls her year of participant observation with the Atlanta police and hopes to conduct a followup study in the near future.